"Darlene and Jake are a
other and God is rocked
cancer concentrate on
lene's primary focus is ⋯   ⋯·-·   ⋯ ⋯· ⋯·⋯⋯·⋯⋯
anxiety-provoking waiting.

"You will be captivated by Darlene's honest and frank disclosures. She deftly describes her own and Jake's responses to waiting and beautifully shares how God answers their cries for help. Her precise use of Scripture is compelling, such that the book sometimes reads as a powerful devotional.

"Readers of this book will better understand the challenges of prostate cancer and likely gain new empathy for those who are 'waiting.'"

—Susan King, BScN

"Darlene and Jake were patients of mine for many years prior to my retirement, and I was involved at the beginning of Jake's cancer. Darlene embraced the theme of being in the waiting room as she and Jake journeyed through his diagnosis, treatment, and continued watching of his cancer. The more I thought of it, it's a very apt metaphor for Jake's journey, but also of ours—even if we don't have cancer. We seem to often be waiting. God sometimes doesn't feel present. But as Darlene points out, God is always there.

"This book is especially suited for families on a cancer journey, but really it's good for all of us who are waiting for God to work in our lives. Darlene's words remind us that God is always waiting with us. His timing is not ours, but He is always sitting with us in our waiting rooms.

"As Jake says repeatedly in the book—and knowing Jake, he says this with firm conviction—'God's got it.'"

—Peter M. Kelton, H.Bsc., M.D.
Family Doctor, Essex County
Former Attending Physician, Erie Shores Health Care, Leamington
Medical Director, Royal Oak Long Term Care, Kingsville

"*The Waiting Room* by Darlene Martens takes us through not only one man's fight against cancer, but also a spiritual one through her own eyes. The impact that the word 'cancer' can have on an individual and the loved ones around them is underestimated. The journey provides spiritual reference, strength, hope, and guidance so they can overcome this difficult chapter in their lives—a chapter that unfortunately finds itself within many families and friends in our community. I commend Darlene in her writing and hope that she doesn't have to be in many more waiting rooms for years to come."

—Dr. Raj Goel, BSc, M.D., FRCS
Urologist

"*The Waiting Room* is a joy to read. It is heart-warming, humorous, touching, sad, difficult, poetic, hopeful, and uplifting all at the same time. We need it!"
—Maria Unger, BRS, Steinbach Bible College,
Pastor's Wife

THE WAITING ROOM

One man's battle with prostate cancer

Darlene Martens

DARLENE MARTENS

THE WAITING ROOM
Copyright © 2024 by Darlene Martens

All rights reserved. Neither this publication nor any part of this publication may be reproduced or transmitted in any form or by any means, electronic or mechanical, including photocopying, recording or any information storage and retrieval system, without permission in writing from the author.

Unless otherwise indicated, all scriptures taken from the Holy Bible, New International Version®, NIV®. Copyright © 1973, 1978, 1984, 2011 by Biblica, Inc.™ Used by permission of Zondervan. All rights reserved worldwide. www.zondervan.com The "NIV" and "New International Version" are trademarks registered in the United States Patent and Trademark Office by Biblica, Inc.™ Scriptures marked (KJV) taken from the Holy Bible, King James Version, which is in the public domain. Scriptures marked (TLB) taken from the Living Bible copyright © 1971 by Tyndale House Foundation. Used by permission of Tyndale House Publishers Inc., Carol Stream, Illinois 60188. All rights reserved. The Living Bible, TLB, and the The Living Bible logo are registered trademarks of Tyndale House Publishers. Scripture quotations taken from the (NASB®) New American Standard Bible®, Copyright © 1960, 1971, 1977, 1995, 2020 by The Lockman Foundation. Used by permission. All rights reserved. lockman.org

Printed in Canada

ISBN: 978-1-4866-2616-8
eBook ISBN: 978-1-4866-2617-5

Word Alive Press
119 De Baets Street Winnipeg, MB R2J 3R5
www.wordalivepress.ca

Cataloguing in Publication information can be obtained from Library and Archives Canada.

This book is dedicated to my dear husband and friend,
Jacob Peter Martens,
affectionately called Jake.

PREFACE

Prostate cancer is the most common cancer among Canadian men (excluding non-melanoma skin cancers). It is the 3rd leading cause of death from cancer in men in Canada...

It is estimated that about 1 in 8 Canadian men will develop prostate cancer during their lifetime and 1 in 30 will die from it.[1]

JAKE WAS DIAGNOSED with prostate cancer in January 2019. This story is about his continuing battle with prostate cancer and its impact on him spiritually, physically, and emotionally, as well as how it impacted us as a couple. The story is also about our relationship with a loving God, who walked with us every step of the way and sat with us in every waiting room. We learned anew the importance of putting our trust and faith in Him.

In the first year of Jake's diagnosis, he had sixty medical appointments, including doctor visits, lab tests, surgery, and radiation treatments. More than one hundred additional appointments have occurred since then. We attended every appointment together and became accustomed to sitting in many waiting rooms.

We also waited between appointments, anxiously anticipating test results and treatments plans. In those periods of waiting, we created figurative waiting rooms in our own minds where we vacillated between fear and trust, anxiety and peace, or worry and waiting on Jesus, the One who gave us the strength to cope and hope.

Amidst all this waiting, we discovered all over again that we didn't need an appointment to talk to God, that we could walk right into His presence

---

[1] "Prostate Cancer Statistics," *Canadian Cancer Society*. May 2024 (https://cancer.ca/en/cancer-information/cancer-types/prostate/statistics).

and lay our heart bare before Him as we cried and sought healing for Jake. God answered our prayer with one word: "Wait." We learned to wait on God and did so with a confident expectation.

In the meantime, as Jake has often declared during this battle, we continue to believe that "God's got it!"

May you be blessed by the Lord's presence as you visit each waiting room along the way.

> Wait for the Lord; be strong and take heart and wait for the Lord. (Psalm 27:14)

I will extol the Lord at all times;
his praise will always be on my lips.
I will glory in the Lord;
let the afflicted hear and rejoice.
Glorify the Lord with me;
let us exalt his name together.
(Psalm 34:1–3)

THE WAITING ROOM

I CLOSED MY eyes and leaned my head on the wall behind me. Male voices resounded in the room as their owners openly shared their urinary and genital health concerns. One man's candidness spawned a frank discussion.

"The doctor told me five years ago that my prostate cancer was terminal," I heard him say. He laughed before adding, confidently, "And here I sit!"

I listened for a few minutes, then tuned out the waiting room chatter. I retreated into a world of my own.

I have no intention of attending these appointments in five years, I told myself. *Because today we will receive good news! Not bad news.*

I wanted to trust my heart's longings, but my gut told me something different. My gut told me that I needed to hope for the best but be prepared for the worst.

I wondered whether Jake was listening to these conversations. I opened my eyes, turned my head, and looked at my husband sitting beside me. He was distracted by the game on his phone, oblivious to what was going on around him and even unaware that I was looking at him.

Rather than disturb him, I returned to my own thoughts.

Until recently, we had never thought much about the prostate gland. We knew the basics, that the prostate gland is the part of the male reproductive system that makes and stores seminal fluid. We had lost some family members to prostate cancer but had never personalized it as something Jake needed to be concerned about.

Over the past year, Jake had struggled with a variety of symptoms including urinary urgency, frequency, and incomplete emptying of his bladder. I often heard him yell, "Get out of my way! I have to pee!" I learned to quickly step aside.

Often, immediately following his rush to go, he had the sudden urge to pee again and would quickly head back to the bathroom.

The Waiting Room

Recurrent pain in his lower back was also a concern. Initially, the doctor thought he had a kidney stone. But tests showed that this wasn't the problem.

Jake also struggled with ongoing but intermittent difficulty with intimacy. This impacted him emotionally. Uncertain as to the cause of the erectile dysfunction (ED), Jake agreed to visit our family doctor. Following a digital rectal examination, the doctor sent him for bloodwork to determine the level of his prostate specific antigen (PSA) and booked him for an ultrasound of his abdomen and kidneys.

Based on the radiologist's recommendation, Jake was referred to see a urologist.

Now, several months following that referral, we sat in the urologist's waiting room.

Waiting.

Waiting for Jake's name to be called.

"Jacob Martens."

We rose.

We followed the voice.

We were led down a hallway and into one of the exam rooms. The room had an exam table and three chairs. In addition, a commode sat in the corner.

Must be common equipment for a urologist's office, I thought.

The nurse asked Jake a number of questions regarding his general health and urinating habits. He then asked Jake to pee into a funnel inside the commode. The nurse explained that the funnel was attached to an electronic device that monitored the urinary output and speed of the urine's flow. In turn, the electronic device produced a printed report which was then provided to the doctor prior to him entering the exam room.

"The doctor will be with you shortly," the nurse said as he stepped out.

Following a brief knock on the door, Dr. King entered. A handsome man, likely in his mid-forties, greeted us in an extremely polite and professional manner. When he shook our hands and smiled, his dark brown eyes met ours. They spoke of care and concern.

Dr. King summarized the findings in the ultrasound report he had received from our family doctor. He then asked me to step out of the room while he did a digital rectal examination to determine whether he could feel a mass on Jake's prostate.

Upon my return, and without explanation, he decisively said, "I would like to do a biopsy. Tomorrow."

There was urgency in his voice. Both Jake and I took quick, deep breaths and swallowed hard.

He then asked us to speak with the booking clerk at the front desk for details regarding the place and time of the biopsy, as well as to obtain a follow-up appointment.

But just as we stepped out of the examining room, Dr. King stopped us.

"Oh but wait," he said. "You're on a blood thinner, aren't you?"

Jake answered in the affirmative. "I'm on a daily dose of baby aspirin."

"Go off the aspirin right away."

He explained that since aspirin thins the blood, he needed to delay the biopsy by two weeks in order to avoid the possibility of bleeding during the procedure.

An immediate sense of frustration arose in us. After all, Dr. King had expressed some urgency about doing the biopsy immediately—yet here we were, having to wait.

We went home and waited.

We were concerned but not alarmed.

Not yet anyway.

> Yes, my soul, find rest in God; my hope comes from him.
> (Psalm 62:5)

THE BIOPSY

THE FRONT DOORS of the hospital opened up to a large and very busy foyer. People were coming and going. Several others waited to register their arrival with the clerk. Jake took a number, then patiently joined the wait.

Once registered, he followed the clerk's directions through a maze of hallways to the day surgery department. I walked by his side. Eight inches taller than me, his height had always provided me with a sense of security. He was my gentle giant, a man of few words, softspoken, kind, and caring.

Once he arrived, he told the clerk that he was there for a biopsy.

"Have a seat," the clerk said matter-of-factly while she motioned to the waiting room. "Someone will come and get you."

I wondered how many times a day she had to say that.

A few minutes later, we heard his name called: "Jacob Martens."

Jake rose and followed the voice.

How interesting, I thought. *Our names really do identify us.*

After all, it wouldn't make sense if the nurse had called John Smith and Jacob Martens rose and followed. Because that wasn't his name. Likewise, it would have been pretty ridiculous if the nurse had called out Jake's name and another man got up to take his place.

For whatever reason, Isaiah 43:1 rang out in my memory: *"Do not fear, for I have redeemed you; I have summoned you by name; you are mine."*

"Fear not." Those two words repeated themselves in my mind.

As Jake walked away from me, I wanted to shout out to him, God says, *"Don't be afraid!"* But I knew my husband well enough to know that he would've been totally embarrassed by any public spectacle. So I bit my tongue and simply savoured the scripture as God's gift to me, intended for that moment in time. It was as if He said to me, *"Don't be afraid, Darlene. I've got it! I've got him!"*

I took a few deep breaths and tried to relax. Before long, I was distracted by the busyness in the room. One woman nodded and smiled at me. I smiled back. She shared about how her broken ankle hadn't healed properly and she now needed some minor surgery. Another, younger woman joined the conversation and told us about her difficult pregnancy.

I sat. I listened. I politely smiled and nodded. I offered the occasional "Is that right?" or "Oh no!"

No one asked me why I was there. I didn't volunteer a reason.

Before I knew it, Jake's biopsy was finished. He later told me that the procedure had been uncomfortable but bearable. He said that it had been just as Dr. King had explained it to us. The doctor inserted a probe into his rectum. With the use of an ultrasound guiding the probe's movements, the doctor took twelve samples of tissue, six from each side of the prostate. Each time a biopsy was taken, Jake heard a click. Since Dr. King had told him that he would take twelve biopsies, Jake had counted the clicks so he would know how close the procedure was to ending.

Prior to doing the biopsy, Dr. King had informed us that there could be possible side effects following the procedure, such as bleeding from the rectum. Fortunately, there were no complications.

We went home.

We waited for the biopsy results.

But we no longer waited in Dr. King's waiting room, nor in the hospital foyer waiting room, nor in the biopsy procedure waiting room. Rather, we were directed to go home and wait. Our home became our waiting room.

Before we knew it, the waiting room moved into our own heads, into our own thoughts. It was a waiting room where I vacillated between fear and faith.

Jake elevated his faith over fear, wholeheartedly believing that God had his best in mind. He trusted God, no matter what.

"God's got it!" Jake confidently said one day during the wait.

He then recalled an experience he had shared with me many years earlier.

"Any time I doubt God's best for me, I remember an experience I had many years ago when I was in the hospital…"

Jake had been admitted to have a kidney stone removed. He had been alone and felt scared, but then a childhood memory had comfortably surfaced. He saw his mother praying on her knees beside her bed. At that thought, he closed his eyes and prayed that God would watch over him.

"Almost immediately, my dark hospital room lit up bright as day and a sense of calm and peace enveloped me," he shared. "I always believed that the presence I saw and felt that night was the Holy Spirit coming to minister to me. That experience never left me. From then on, I knew that any time when things felt dark and worrisome, I could lean on my faith. It never falters."

So we waited in waiting rooms of our own making.

I sat in my waiting room where fear fought faith, Jake in his waiting room where faith faced fear.

We prayed while we waited.

We asked others to pray.

While we waited in the waiting.

> Prayer: Lord Jesus, thank You for being an all-caring God. Thank You for caring about Jake. Thank You that the biopsy went well today. Now, Lord, our hope and prayer is that Jake doesn't have cancer. We ask that we will receive good news. In Jesus's precious name we pray, amen.

WAITING LONGER

JAKE HAD A follow-up appointment scheduled two weeks after the biopsy. We tried to keep busy while waiting for the biopsy report. We worked, cooked, cleaned, shopped, spent time with our children and friends, and did a myriad of other normal things. When we kept ourselves physically busy, our minds were also occupied.

But when we weren't busy, our thoughts ran wild. At those times, it felt like fear and worry grabbed us by the ankles and pulled us down into a quagmire where our feet couldn't seem to find solid ground.

The worst time of day was bedtime, when our minds were no longer kept busy and focused. At bedtime, we needed to rest and could only do so if we shut out the worries of the day, specifically the worry about Jake potentially having prostate cancer.

Unfortunately, that was when fear and worry either prevented us from falling asleep or screamed at us like a blaring alarm, jolting us awake when we stirred in the middle of the night.

"Remember us!" they shouted. "We're still here! Your problem hasn't gone away!"

We eventually shared our hearts with each other.

"I'm so afraid you have cancer." My voice shook as I spoke. "And I worry about how that will change your life, and our lives together."

Jake replied to me calmly and lovingly. "Let's not go there. Once we know, we'll know. The fact is that at this point in time I've had a biopsy and we don't know anything else."

He tried so hard to remain positive.

Although I heard what Jake said, my thoughts finished his statement by adding: yet.

But over that two-week period, Jake admitted that his thoughts also often jumped to the worst possible outcome. At those times, he turned to

The Waiting Room

his faith to calm himself down. He told me that he simply reassured himself with his foundational belief: "God's got it!"

I wished I could have been that confident.

The day prior to his follow-up appointment, Jake received a telephone call from the doctor's office. They needed to reschedule his appointment to the new year. Apparently, the doctor hadn't yet received the biopsy report due to a backlog in the health records department.

Our hearts sank.

The changed appointment meant waiting longer.

Waiting longer meant waiting over the holidays.

I felt emotionally charged. Fear ran wild in my thoughts and then exploded out of my mouth: "Waiting over the holidays means our Christmas will be ruined! It must mean you'll be getting bad news. After all, if it was good news, she might've told you that everything was okay and the doctor would see you in a year for a checkup."

Jake had been trying to stay positive, and when he replied he was understandably slightly perturbed by my heightened emotional state.

"We have one fact to go on and that is this: there was a delay in receiving the report." He spoke firmly. "I actually feel relieved that the office postponed my appointment. Can you imagine how our holiday might be ruined if we knew I had cancer?"

In an effort not to discourage him, I kept my next thought to myself: *But just imagine how wonderful our holiday could be if we knew you didn't have cancer!*

Due to no fault of our own, we had been directed back to a waiting room. Unfortunately, it was a waiting room where fear and worry lurked and demanded our attention, especially mine. Since we knew that fear wasn't of God, we intentionally tried to place our faith over that fear and worry.

> For God hath not given us the spirit of fear; but of power, and of love, and of a sound mind. (2 Timothy 1:7, KJV)

We also became acutely aware that fear was the root cause of the anxiety I felt. This caused us to lean into the promise that He was near, that we didn't need to be anxious, and that we could go to Him in prayer.

> The Lord is near. Do not be anxious about anything, but in every situation, by prayer and petition, with thanksgiving, present your requests to God. And the peace of God, which transcends all understanding, will guard your hearts and your minds in Christ Jesus. (Philippians 4:5–7)
>
> Cast all your anxiety on him because he cares for you. (1 Peter 5:7)
>
> Come to me, all you who are weary and burdened, and I will give you rest. Take my yoke upon you and learn from me, for I am gentle and humble in heart, and you will find rest for your souls. For my yoke is easy and my burden is light. (Matthew 11:28–30)

We knew those verses. We knew He was near. We knew we could go to Him. We knew we could give Him our anxiety. We also knew He carried us and cared about us. We knew that when we gave Him our anxiety, we were also giving Him our fear. We knew that we needed to put our trust in Him and totally believe the truth: "God's got it!"

But.

It wasn't easy.

Some days we felt strong emotionally. On those days, we entered the waiting room of prayer, presented our requests to God, and parked our anxiety at His feet. We simply put our faith in Him. Then we busied ourselves with other things.

But other days we left the waiting room of faith and opened the door to the waiting room across the hall. There, we rubbed shoulders with fear and worry. There, our human weaknesses and thoughts kept getting in the way of casting our anxiety on Him.

Oh how we wished we could have put a lock on that waiting room door!

> Prayer: Lord Jesus, we praise You for being an all-knowing God. You know exactly what we feel, even before we feel it. Forgive us, Lord, for those times when we forget

to focus on our faith in You, when we allow our fear to take over. Lord, please help us to put our faith over that fear and worry that causes us so much anxiety. In Jesus's name we pray, amen.

THE NEWS

"For I know the plans I have for you," declares the Lord, "plans to prosper you and not to harm you, plans to give you hope and a future. Then you will call on me and come and pray to me, and I will listen to you. You will seek me and find me when you seek me with all your heart." (Jeremiah 29:11–13)

IT WAS A cold January day when we headed into the city for Jake's appointment. As far as the eye could see, the open fields glistened from the sun's reflection on the snow. We were grateful that the country roads were free and clear.

As before, we wove our way through the hospital corridors to the urologist's office. Jake registered with the clerk and we took a seat across the hall in the waiting room. It was a waiting room I had hoped to never see again.

Unlike the first day we'd sat here, there were fewer people talking. The conversation felt like a soft drone in the background.

Rather than listen to the chatter, I played games on my phone.

"Jacob Martens."

Together we rose and followed the voice. We were led across the hall, down a hallway, and into an exam room where we waited for the doctor. This particular room had a colourful wall chart of the male reproductive system and urinary tract. The male anatomy was meticulously labelled, including the prostate.

"There it is!" I said to Jake, pointing to the prostate. "That walnut-sized organ in front of the rectum and just below the bladder."

Jake smiled and simply nodded, apparently much less intrigued than I was by this detail.

I continued as I returned to my chair. "Well! If nothing else, this has certainly been an education!"

An education I could've easily lived without, I mumbled to myself under my breath.

We held hands while we sat in silence.

Dr. King entered and once again greeted us in his very friendly and personable manner, saying that it was good to see us again. We both nodded in agreement.

I swallowed my feelings and didn't verbalize my next thought: *It would be good to see you again... if we were in a different place under different circumstances.*

Dr. King spoke calmly as he reiterated the purpose of the appointment: to let us know the results of the recent biopsy. Although I knew he was doing his job, I felt impatience and anxiety rise up in me.

Yes, we are aware of this! Now get on with it! Just tell us already!

We listened politely as he explained the concerning symptoms of an elevated PSA, his ability to palpate a mass on the right side of the prostate and his decision to do a biopsy.

We then heard him say it.

"Unfortunately, the biopsy shows that it is cancer." He paused while he took a breath. "But the good news is..."

I didn't hear the rest of that sentence. I was distracted by his words. I tried to process what they meant.

Good news? I asked myself. *How is it that he can use the word cancer and yet somehow equate it with good news? All in the same sentence!*

I wanted to scream. Not at Dr. King. I wanted to scream at the news. At the cancer.

I suddenly felt frustrated with myself. After all, I considered myself skilled at teaching people to look for the silver lining in the middle of a dark cloud, or to change negative ways of thinking to positive, or to be able to improve one's self-talk.

Yet there I was, required to find a silver lining. I couldn't find one positive thought to counterbalance the fact that Jake had just been diagnosed with prostate cancer.

The News

I wished I hadn't been able to think of all these other things when I was supposed to be listening. I told myself that I needed to stay alert. I couldn't get stuck on the word cancer.

I looked over at Jake and could tell from the blank look on his face that he had shut down and retreated into a world of his own.

I tried my best to put my feelings aside. I feverishly wrote down what the doctor was saying while my brain desperately tried to separate my emotions from the task at hand.

Dr. King briefly explained the Gleason score, a way to evaluate abnormal prostate cancer cells and their potential of spreading. The biopsy results showed Jake's Gleason score to be a 7, or a medium-grade cancer with an intermediate risk of spreading. Although it wasn't the best news, it was presented to us in such a positive light that it felt like we should see this as a good thing.

"You have two options at this point in time," Dr. King continued. "One is radiation therapy, and the other is major surgery to remove the prostate. I've already booked an appointment for you to see a doctor at the cancer clinic. He's a radiation oncologist and will take you through the necessary steps should you decide to do radiation."

Dr. King explained that since prostate cancer can metastasize to the bones or lymph nodes, it was necessary to get a more complete diagnosis. Jake had therefore been scheduled for a bone scan to rule out any bone involvement, as well as a CAT scan to rule out any lymph node involvement. Should both these tests prove negative, the next step would be to do radiation or surgery.

On the other hand, should either one of the tests be positive, we would talk about the next steps at Jake's follow-up appointment in about six weeks' time.

We rose and thanked the doctor for his kindness. We didn't thank him for the bad news.

The clerk booked a date for the bone and CAT scans. She then asked us to stop at the pharmacy on our way out of the hospital to pick up a bottle of barium sulphate, used as a contrast agent in preparation for CAT scans.

We headed to the pharmacy and waited for the people in line ahead of us to be accommodated.

The Waiting Room

I suddenly felt ill to my stomach. My head spun. I knew it was a visceral reaction to all the information we had just been given. In addition, I felt annoyed that we now needed to pay forty dollars on this gross barium sulphate. It felt like we were being sucker-punched while we were already down.

My deep thoughts and mixed emotions were suddenly interrupted by the pleasant young woman behind the counter. I told her what we wanted.

"Would you like chocolate or vanilla flavoured?" she asked sweetly.

I replied politely, but my insides screamed. *Are you kidding me! He has a choice?* Then sarcasm joined the chorus. *He really has no choice, now does he?*

I smiled at the young woman, paid for the bottle, and politely thanked her as we left.

We left the hospital feeling numb.

We held hands as we walked together to the car.

> Prayer: Lord Jesus, we don't even know how to pray right now except to ask You to comfort us, help us to process the news we received today, and give us the needed direction as we move forward. In Jesus's name we pray, amen.

WE HAVE SOMETHING TO TELL YOU

I will extol the Lord at all times; his praise will always be on my lips. (Psalm 34:1)

APPROXIMATELY TEN YEARS prior to Jake's diagnosis, our son-in-law was diagnosed with colon cancer. He and our daughter lived about ten minutes from our home. They decided that his family would be the first to receive news about his health, after which they would notify us before anything was posted on social media.

At that time, our middle daughter lived in Alberta with her husband, and our youngest daughter lived in South Korea. With all of our girls living in different time zones, they needed to develop three-way communication at unusual hours in order to make that information-sharing happen.

Jake and I decided to follow our children's example and ensure that any news about Jake's health would be shared first with our adult children before anyone else.

From the car, we called our daughters and sons-in-law to tell them the results of the biopsy. Following a bit of small talk, the conversation shifted. We shared the little fact that their father did indeed have prostate cancer, that we didn't yet know a prognosis, and that he had been referred to an oncologist. We also told them that we needed to decide whether to go with either radiation or surgery. We valued their input.

Every phone call ended with a reciprocal "Love you!" and these were no exception.

The more often we shared the bad news, the more real it became. As the reality hit home, the more it impacted us.

Interestingly enough, however, the more it impacted us, the more I noticed Jake's faith surface. He confidently and calmly declared, "No matter what, God's got it!" Eventually, this turned into a decision and commitment to continue praising God for all He had done for us—no matter what.

PRAISE HIM ANYWAY

MANY YEARS PRIOR to this, I found myself blaming God for all the horrible things that had happened in my life. I yelled and screamed at Him and even believed that I needed to forgive Him. This meant, of course, that I believed He'd done something wrong.

When I recognized my faulty thinking, I went on a journey to discover who God is. In that process, He never stopped loving me. He was patient with me and recognized my human frailty and brutal honesty. As I learned more about Him, He also taught me more about myself and my need for a holy Saviour.

At the end of that journey, I discovered that God had done nothing wrong.

I identified many of God's attributes in His Word. This is not an exhaustive list, but it does identify many of His wonderful characteristics.

Psalm 139 taught me that God is all-knowing, all-powerful, and present everywhere.

As outlined by David in Psalm 103, I learned that God forgives, heals, redeems, crowns us with love and compassion, satisfies our desires with good things, and is right and just for the oppressed, compassionate, gracious, slow to anger, and abounding in love. He has removed our sins, loves us, removes our transgressions, has compassion on those who fear Him, and now sits on His throne in heaven.

At the end of this psalm, David reiterates that God's love for us is everlasting.

> But from everlasting to everlasting the Lord's love is with those who fear him... (Psalm 103:17)

The New Testament also told me that God is love (1 John 4:16). And I discovered that both the Old and New Testaments indicate that God doesn't change.

> Jesus Christ is the same yesterday and today and forever. (Hebrews 13:8)
>
> In the beginning you laid the foundations of the earth, and the heavens are the work of your hands. They will perish, but you remain... But you remain the same, and your years will never end. (Psalm 102:25, 27)

Since God doesn't change, His attributes also don't change; they remain the same. This meant that I could always count on who God is and who God says He is, since they are the very essence and nature of His character.

This helped me to recognize that He wasn't to blame for those bad things that have happened in my life. Furthermore, He wasn't to blame for the cancer Jake now faced.

Knowing God's unchangeable qualities changed my worship time with the Lord because I felt that I could truly praise Him rather than being upset about something I thought He had done to me or to us. I knew that I could:

> Shout for joy to the Lord, all the earth. Worship the Lord with gladness; come before him with joyful songs... Enter his gates with thanksgiving and his courts with praise; give thanks to him and praise his name. For the Lord is good and his love endures forever; his faithfulness continues through all generations. (Psalm 100:1–2, 4–5)

Jake had been aware of my struggle. So when I shared my new understanding with him, he immediately joined me in rejoicing in the Lord always (Philippians 4:4).

While we waited.

Prayer: Dear Jesus, we praise You. We praise You for who You are. We praise You for being a God who loves, forgives, and is just, compassionate, and slow to anger. We thank You for being a God who never changes. We thank You for loving us. When we feel down about the things that have happened in our lives, please remind us to turn our eyes toward You. Help us to praise You, no matter what, even when we might be in the depth of despair. In Jesus's name we pray, amen.

NO APPOINTMENT NEEDED

> Wait for the Lord; be strong and take heart and wait for the Lord. (Psalm 27:14)

FOR SEVERAL YEARS I worked as a social worker for the walk-in counselling clinic at our local hospital. This service was vital for those in mental health crises, giving them the opportunity to process their thoughts and feelings about relationships, depression, and anxiety, amongst other issues. Attending was simple. There was no need for an appointment.

Jake and I went into crisis mode the very moment Dr. King first said Jake had cancer. Although it wasn't a prognosis of imminent death, that word threw us into the unknown. In the midst of Jake's faith and confidence, our emotions spiralled out of control. All the what-ifs taunted us. Wonder and worry slapped us in the face with fear. Doubt sneered at us with a myriad of unanswered questions.

We had faced troubles in the past, including crop failures, financial difficulties, health issues, mental health battles, and the loss of loved ones. At those times, we had gone to the Lord for support.

We knew we could go to Him again. We also knew that the sign on His door read "No Appointment Needed." Without a doubt, we could walk right into His presence and He would meet with us.

So when we arrived home that day, we walked into the office of our Great Physician. No appointment necessary. He took us right in.

> Come to me, all you who are weary and burdened, and I will give you rest. Take my yoke upon you and learn from me, for I am gentle and humble in heart, and you will find rest for your souls. For my yoke is easy and my burden is light. (Matthew 11:28–30)

Both Jake and I sat with God. Separately. I called out to Him while in my office. Jake later told me he cried out to Him while in our bedroom.

While we individually met with Him, He ministered to us with love. As we shared our fears and hurts with Him, we felt His love surround us. He held us. Close. We wept while in His presence. We wept in His arms. We committed the unknown to Him. We laid our burdens down at His feet. He promised He would carry us as we felt Him encourage us that there would be a time when we'd learn to walk on our own.

We told Him that we didn't want to travel down this path called cancer, but He promised us that He would be with us every step of the way. We asked for healing.

"Wait."

He asked us to wait for His answer and directed us to His waiting room. Jesus sat with us there.

> Prayer: Dear Jesus, we praise and thank You for always being there—any time, night or day. Thank You, Lord, for always waiting for us. I guess it means You love us! We ask for You to heal Jake, to make him better. In Jesus's name we pray, amen.

THE JOURNEY OF LIFE

IN HIS EARLY twenties, Jake and three of his buddies travelled together to the Muskoka region in northern Ontario for a week-long canoe and portage trip. They enjoyed the peaceful and beautiful scenery abundantly laid before them, complete with magnificent oak, elm, and maple trees standing tall and strong. They appreciated the variety of evergreens, inland lakes, and blue rivers.

Several weeks of planning had led up to this trip, including which lakes they would take, where they would portage, and what they should bring in terms of food and other supplies: canoes, paddles, life jackets, tents, sleeping bags, clothes, etc.

After a five-hour drive, they finally arrived at one of their family's cottages. From there, they headed out for their canoe trip, which took them onto Lake Muskoka, Mary's Lake, and Lake of Bays. For the most part, their portage times from one lake to another were short, although one portage took several hours to complete over rough terrain.

The beginning of the canoe trip was difficult because they had to fight against the current and then head uphill during portages. Jake recalled that the second half was easier because they canoed with the current and headed downhill during portages. They had packed light so they could easily carry their canoes and supplies during portages. This also made paddling easier, as long as it wasn't windy and the water was still.

Each day brought something different, including a mixture of fun and challenges.

At one point, a sense of panic and fear surged through them when a man sped by them in a motor boat in an effort to swamp them. Fortunately, they stayed upright.

In another situation, one of their canoes got caught in some rapids while going from one section of the lake to another. They'd ended up getting hung up on a large stone. Fortunately, they were able to repair a hole in the bottom of the canoe and once again head out onto the water.

On yet another occasion, they went ashore for the night. With nowhere else to sleep, they had to pitch their tent under a no-trespassing sign.

It amazed them at how much God provided for them during these experiences.

Another evening, when they went ashore to set up camp for the night, they came across a restaurant not far from their camp sight. Although the restaurant was closed, the owner was nearby and welcomed them to go inside and use the kitchen to heat up their food.

One day, while walking through the woods, they came across a freshwater spring as it bubbled up from the ground. Its random location spoke to them of a God who provides.

Each night they enjoyed building a campfire, eating mac and cheese or beans and wieners, and chatting while they enjoyed the beautiful starlit sky.

As Jake recalled this canoe trip with its fun and challenges, he told me that it felt like it was representative of the journey we go through in life. Every day they entered the unfamiliar, a world of the unknown, and had to rely on the provision and protection of the Lord.

"It's just like going through this battle with cancer. Each day we go into the unknown." He confidently added, "From as far back as I can remember, I have always known that the Lord was with me. There have been many times in my life when I relied on His presence and protection. Our canoe trip was one of those such times. Cancer has been another."

Jake then recalled Moses's encouraging words to Joshua as he passed along the leadership baton in front of all of Israel:

> Be strong and courageous, for you must go with this people into the land that the Lord swore to their ancestors to give them, and you must divide it among them as their inheritance. The Lord himself goes before you and will be with you; he will never leave you nor forsake you. Do not be afraid; do not be discouraged. (Deuteronomy 31:7–8)

Likewise, as we stepped forward into this world of the unknown called cancer, we knew we weren't alone. We knew that the Lord would go before us.

While we waited.

> Prayer: Dear Jesus, we praise and thank You for how You have created our world. So beautiful! We also thank You for Your ongoing protection over us during our journey through life. Please give us the courage now to remember that You go ahead of us, that You will be with us, and that You will not leave us. Help us to be strong and courageous, especially in those times when we face the unknown in this battle against cancer. Thanks again, Lord, for loving us. In Jesus's name we pray, amen.

RADIATION VS. SURGERY

> I waited patiently for the Lord; he turned to me and heard my cry. (Psalm 40:1)

WE HAD DRIVEN by the regional cancer centre many times. We were aware of its existence and the work done there but had never really given it a second thought—that is, until it became personal. We were weighed down with a variety of emotions as we walked towards the cancer centre. Apprehension joined us, along with sadness, fear of the unknown, worry, and even dread.

But the moment we walked through its doors, the centre's very essence came to life. Its friendly volunteers and professional staff calmed our fears while offering hope.

At the time, we didn't know that the cancer centre would eventually become a familiar place, although it was a familiarity we'd have happily lived without.

Jake registered at the front desk while I stepped aside and took in my surroundings.

"Have a seat in the waiting room. Someone will be with you shortly." The receptionist handed Jake a thin white binder that contained an assortment of pages full of information about medicine, pain management, dietitians, social workers, symptom management, as well as a variety of other services and programs offered there.

For whatever reason, I had always been Jake's official "stuff" holder, and it was no different on this particular day. Jake passed the binder on to me and I carried it to the waiting room.

When we sat down, I handed the binder back to him.

"My purse isn't big enough!" I said, chuckling as I held up my small handbag.

When I returned the binder to him, however, I caught a glimpse of the title on its cover: My Cancer Journey. My insides flipped and I felt my blood pressure rise.

Journey? I thought with a scowl. *Journey?!*

I abruptly stood and walked away.

I wanted to run.

I needed to process the anger that surged in me.

I stormed down the hospital corridor.

I flailed my arms while I talked to myself.

I was exasperated!

This isn't a journey! A journey is something I plan. It's something we plan. Like a vacation, or a hike, or even a day together. We have control. We make the decisions. We plan what roads to take and where we'll eat. We decide how fast we drive and when we want to stop. We choose the hotels to sleep in and what time we'll rise in the morning.

My steps picked up speed. I felt so irritated.

This isn't a journey! It's more like a dream gone bad. It's a nightmare full of fear, fear of the unknown with so many twists and turns. The hospital is so large that half the time we don't know the way to an office, lab, or pharmacy. We're constantly asking for directions. Where's the bathroom? Which way to the oncology department? What waiting room do we sit in?'

My thoughts and my feelings spun out of control. I felt like a fly caught in a spiderweb and I couldn't get free.

I had to find a way to compose myself knowing that Jake would need me when his name was called. I had no option but to push the anger, confusion, and angst down to a place in my heart where they couldn't control me. At least not at the moment. Down to a place where I could deal with them in my own way, in my own time.

I nearly choked as I took a deep breath and swallowed hard. I returned to my seat. I didn't share my mini mental breakdown with Jake; he needed me to be alert and strong.

"Jacob Martens."

Together we rose and followed the voice. We travelled down a maze of hallways and were directed into an exam room. The nurse took Jake's blood pressure and weight before again asking him a number of questions, including his birthdate.

The oncologist was very kind. He told us that he had reviewed the reports from the urologist, including the pathology report from the biopsy.

"I'll have to develop a treatment plan specific for how the radiation would be focused on your prostate," he told Jake.

Our understanding of radiation treatments had been informed by a pamphlet we'd been given by the urologist. It explained that high-energy radiation would be produced by a special machine called a linear accelerator. Those beams would focus on the prostate from different angles on a daily basis for several weeks.

We asked questions regarding the difference between radiation and surgery, specifically as it related to the long-term prognosis. We also asked questions regarding the long-term side effects of radiation.

The oncologist did his best to answer our questions. He also suggested that we keep Jake's next appointment with the urologist and ask him the same questions.

Before we left, he reassured us that he would be there to help should we choose to pursue radiation.

While we waited for Jake's next appointment with the urologist, we did our own research regarding the pros and cons of radiation and surgery.

We discovered that even though surgery was more invasive, the upside was that there would be a greater chance to remove all the cancer cells. As well, tissue could be removed to help the pathologist determine whether the cancer had spread outside the capsule of the prostate. We also discovered that removing the prostate after undergoing radiation would be very difficult, since the radiation would leave the prostate in a fragile state.

"Well, I have good news!" the urologist declared at Jake's follow-up appointment. "The bone scan and CAT scan were both clear."

That news led us into a discussion regarding our next steps. Dr. King confirmed that radiation was a simpler form of treatment and less invasive than a complete prostatectomy. However, the benefits of surgery included the potential of getting all the cancer and generating a pathology report to assist in determining future treatment.

Based on this information, together with Jake's elevated PSA, the biopsy report, and the Gleason score, we decided that surgery was needed to remove the prostate. It seemed like the best treatment option for us.

We waited for a surgery date.

> Prayer: Dear Jesus, we praise You for who You are, for being a God who knows, a God who is always there, and a God who heals. Thank You that Jake's cancer hasn't been found in the lymph nodes or his bones. That's such good news! We continue to ask for healing, and while we wait please help us to not lean on ourselves but acknowledge You as the sustainer of life as You direct our decisions concerning what's best for him. In Jesus's name we pray, amen.

A FIRM FOUNDATION

THE AMBASSADOR BRIDGE spans the Detroit River and connects Windsor, Ontario to Detroit, Michigan. The bridge was completed and opened in November 1929 at the beginning of the Great Depression.

This bridge is considered to be the busiest international crossing between Canada and the United States with more than ten thousand trucks and four thousand cars crossing on a daily basis. The bridge provides access to travellers and supports commerce on both sides of the border.

With the anticipation of needing to account for future growth in international commerce and trade, and following a lot of controversy and bureaucracy on both sides of the border, a second bridge was planned for. Its construction commenced in 2018. Four tall towers, two on each side of the river, will support the new bridge in its two-and-a-half-kilometre span over the water. Standing 151 feet above the Detroit River, in order to allow for ships to pass underneath, the bridge will connect Interstate 75 in the United States to Highway 401 in Canada.[2]

This bridge, the Gordie Howe International Bridge, has been rightly named in honour of Gordie Howe, a Canadian born in Floral, Saskatchewan. Also known as Mr. Hockey, his twenty-five-year career as a right-wing player for the Detroit Red Wings helped lead the team to the Stanley Cup four times in the early 1950s.

Since construction began, we have occasionally driven by the site in order to get a closer view of its progress. Initially we saw the four corner posts go up, two on each side of the river. It then took approximately three years to appropriately place the towers. Each tower is 722 feet tall and supported by six shafts drilled thirty-six metres into the bedrock.

---

[2] "Project Profile: Gordie Howe International Bridge," *U.S. Department of Transportation*. Date of access: July 9, 2024 (https://www.fhwa.dot.gov/ipd/project_profiles/mi_gordie_howe_int_bridge.aspx).

One article we read provided a visual of this. That's the equivalent of an eleven-story building.

Since the rest of the bridge will be supported by these towers, it's essential that the towers are solid and secure in their foundations. This allows the bridge to stand strong, giving it the strength to stand up against winds and storms as well as the weight of trucks and other traffic that crosses on a daily basis.

Over time, the roadways were laid in place and attached to the towers of the cable stays. Eventually we saw the construction of approaches on both sides of the river. At one point, we wondered what would happen if the two ends didn't meet in the middle, or if one end of the road turned out to be lower than the other.

Amazingly, five years after the beginning of the construction of the bridge, the news recently showed a Canadian construction worker shaking hands with his American counterpart at the point where the two sides of the bridge join together at the middle of the river. It was a proud moment.

We marvelled at this manmade structure, confident that since the Ambassador Bridge has stood strong for nearly a century, the new technology used in the building of the Gordie Howe International Bridge will also cause it to stand strong.

This reminds us of the biblical account of the wise man who built his house on the rock.

> Therefore everyone who hears these words of mine and puts them into practice is like a wise man who built his house on the rock. The rain came down, the streams rose, and the winds blew and beat against that house; yet it did not fall, because it had its foundation on the rock. (Matthew 7:24–25)

Because that man built his house on the rock, his house stood strong.

As we look back over our lives, we can also marvel at how we have been able to withstand the many storms in our lives only because we built our lives on Jesus Christ, the firm foundation.

> For no one can lay any foundation other than the one already laid, which is Jesus Christ. (1 Corinthians 3:11)

Because we built our lives on this firm foundation, we know that even though there will be difficult times, we'll be able to withstand any future storms of life as they come our way, including cancer. This has given us strength and encouragement as we build our hope on the solid Rock, Jesus Christ.

While we wait.

> Prayer: Dear Jesus, we thank and praise You for being the firm foundation of our lives. We know that without You we would be unable to survive the winds and storms of life, in particular this storm called cancer. Help us to lean on You as our solid Rock in those times when we face discouragement. In Jesus's name we pray, amen.

FLORIDA

THIRTY YEARS EARLIER, on a cold, bright, and sunny day in February 1989, we picked up our young daughters from school. When they got in the car, we told them that instead of going home we were on our way to catch a plane that would take us to Disney World in Florida.

Understandably, they didn't believe us.

Each one had different questions regarding their clothes, missing school, and who would take care of our family dog while we were away. We took the time they needed to alleviate their concerns, then headed out on our journey.

Our time in Florida was amazing. We explored Orlando, ate every meal in a restaurant, swam in the hotel pool, went to Disney World, and had a lot of great old-fashioned fun. Together.

"It's a Small World After All" was one of the girls' favourite rides, but by the end of the week Jake grew tired of listening to that "kiddy" song over and over again. After all, his love for music had always centred around Abba, the Beach Boys, and Christian rock.

Many years later, though, he admitted to having enjoyed the ride mostly because the girls had liked it so much.

We built wonderful memories that week, so much so that one of our daughters called in the early part of 2018 to say that she had talked to her sisters and they were hoping we could go again as a family. The biggest difference was that our family had grown from a group of five to a group of thirteen.

"But it will be so much fun!" she implored.

We put a plan in place to go in February 2019.

Given that thirty years had passed, I decided that I needed a professional trip planner for this trip. I packed up my preliminary research, along with a list of questions, and headed to our local travel agency. I prayed that someone there would have the necessary experience and knowledge to help me.

When I arrived, I was immediately greeted by our pastor's wife, who told me that she was considered the Disney World expert. With her help, as well as input from Jake and our adult children, we planned the best trip ever.

Just six weeks after Jake's diagnosis, eight of us flew together to Florida. We settled into our hotel and waited for the others to arrive from Alberta. I will always remember standing together in the parking lot of our hotel as we watched for them to arrive.

We watched, we expected, and we anticipated.

We leaned into hope that they would arrive safely.

We were overjoyed when we finally saw them, so excited to finally be together as a family. It was certainly a fait accomplis!

For the next full week, we ate, played, and laughed together. We hugged, loved, and cherished each other. Everyone ate candy, but some wanted more. The children had permission to have orange soda with their meals, and then they wanted more. We enjoyed the exhibits and rides.

Just as we had experienced thirty years previous, the waits in line for a ride were often up to two hours long. But nobody seemed to mind because there was a quiet understanding that Disney World didn't have any bad rides. Knowing that made the wait tolerable.

At the end of each day, the rooms grew quiet and everyone slept soundly in anticipation of the beginning of another new day. Together.

At the end of the week, Jake commented on how marvellous it was that we hadn't had any disagreements or tears. There had only been one occasion when we heard our four-year old granddaughter sassing her father. I heard her say to him, "No! I don't have to, because I'm a princess!" He replied, "You aren't acting like a princess! Princesses are kind and cooperative!" She then grew quiet and cooperated with her father.

It was a wonderful week together. We have often declared that it was the best vacation ever. But to me and Jake, it was a gift to have been together as a family, especially just weeks after his cancer diagnosis.

> I wait for the Lord, my whole being waits, and in his word
> I put my hope. (Psalm 130:5)

SURGERY DAY

SIX WEEKS AFTER returning home, Jake was scheduled for a robot-assisted radical prostatectomy. The process was akin to laparoscopic surgery, except that the video camera and instruments were linked to a robotic system controlled by the surgeon.

As we prepared to leave for the hospital, Jake watched me place a bag in the car with a few of his personal belongings. When I placed a second bag in the car, he became curious.

"What's in the other bag?" he asked.

"Just a few things for me to eat. A sandwich, a drink, and some snacks." I sighed deeply, my heart heavy with concern for my husband. "It will be a long day!"

Jake chuckled. "Yup! And I get to sleep for most of it!"

We both laughed.

It was a cool April 1 morning. The skies were clear yet still dark when we pulled out of our laneway.

We both felt at peace about the surgery and resigned to the fact that it was necessary in order to prolong his life. We made small talk as we headed into the city.

As had become our custom, we prayed before we got out of the car at the hospital. We committed our concerns and anxiety to Him and asked the Lord to protect Jake. He then registered at the reception desk in the foyer, after which we followed the directions to the surgical wing.

Jake approached the clerk and introduced himself in a very light-hearted manner—by his birthday: "May 3, 1948!"

The nurse looked at him, cocked her head, and smiled. With a twinkle in her eye, she asked for his name.

The Waiting Room

The joke certainly brought her a bit of joy so early in the morning, but it was also evidence to us of the peace Jake felt. He was confident that he was in the Lord's care.

After finding his name in the computer, the clerk directed us to have a seat in the waiting room.

A few minutes later, we heard his name called: "Jacob Martens."

Funny. I chuckled. *Why didn't they just call out his birthdate?*

Jake stood to follow. As he did, he squeezed my hand and we shared a quick kiss.

While he walked away, the clerk gave me a piece of paper with a number written on it and directed me to a different waiting room designated for family members of surgical patients. I easily located the room, although it was very full. I found one empty seat on the far side of the room and settled in.

Strange, I thought to myself as I sat. *How is it that a person can sit in a crowded room and yet feel so alone?*

I took a deep breath and slowly exhaled while scanning the room. Everyone's face seemed so serious. No one was smiling. Some seemed sad. The tension was almost tangible.

I also noticed that it appeared as though everyone was with someone. No one else was alone.

Two are better than one, I thought, then remembered Solomon's words in Ecclesiastes:

> Though one may be overpowered, two can defend themselves. A cord of three strands is not quickly broken. (Ecclesiastes 4:12)

God had always been that third strand in our marriage and I knew that this day it would be no different. I took comfort in knowing that He was with me in the waiting room, and in this waiting.

I was not alone.

When I looked around the room again, I noticed that many people were focused on a large television mounted on the wall. I looked up, expecting to see a morning news show and instead was met with a scrolling list of numbers. Next to them were surgical status updates.

Well, that explained the number the nurse had handed me. What an ingenious way to keep people informed about their loved ones!

I found Jake's number on the screen and watched for any change in his status.

When *In surgery* popped up on the screen, fear and dread stirred within me. I took another deep breath and quietly prayed for Jake, for his nerves, for the hands of the surgeon and the equipment he would use. I quietly prayed that I could remain calm and not be afraid.

Out of the corner of my eye, I noticed two familiar people as they entered. It wasn't my sister's short hair and my brother's full beard that caught my attention, as much as it was their smiling faces. It felt good to have them there as support.

"We didn't want you to be alone," they lovingly stated.

For the next hour or so, we talked about our families and laughed as we recalled some childhood memories. They stood to leave when our girls arrived.

I had anticipated that our youngest daughter would arrive shortly but was doubly blessed when our eldest daughter joined her despite having worked all night. Hellos, hugs, inquiries, and goodbyes seemed to pass simultaneously between the girls and their aunt and uncle.

I explained the scrolling board to the girls and shared Jake's number with them. We made small talk while we waited.

Several hours later, we noticed the board change. First, *Out of surgery*. Then, *In recovery*.

Before long, Dr. King entered the waiting room and asked us to join him in a small board room. He told us that he had successfully removed Jake's prostate. He then drew the male reproductive system on a nearby whiteboard and pointed out the location of the prostate gland.

"Prior to going into surgery, we were aware that there was a mass on the right side of the prostate," he explained. "We were able to safely remove the mass. However, the cancer wasn't encapsulated in the prostate. Rather, the cancer had broken through the wall of the prostate and as a result we also had to take some tissue from around the prostate. Unfortunately…"

The Waiting Room

That's when my brain shut down. I heard what he was saying, but my ears fought with my heart. From experience, I was fully aware that bad news usually followed the word unfortunately.

Dr. King continued. "It appeared the cancer had already spread into the seminal vesicles, and as a result these were also surgically removed. In addition, I removed a lymph node in order to help us determine whether the cancer had spread into the lymphatic system."

It was a lot to absorb and he took time to answer our questions.

Our oldest daughter, knowing well what I was experiencing, asked the doctor whether her father would need to have chemo in the future. Dr. King explained that he was unable to answer that just yet.

"Let's wait and see what the pathology report tells us. Then we'll go from there."

Overall, it was certainly a good news/bad news kind of day. Jake was out of surgery safe and sound, but the doctor's findings horrified me.

"Have a seat in the waiting room," Dr. King said. "A nurse will take you down to recovery shortly."

I thanked him for taking such good care of my husband.

We sat quietly while I tried to process all the information. Once again I had to wait.

> Prayer: Lord Jesus, I thank You and praise You for being in the operating room with Jake and the surgical team. Thank You for the skilled hands that cared for my husband today. Thank You for him coming safely through surgery. Help me to continue to trust in You, especially at those times when we receive bad news. Please continue to protect him. And again I ask for complete healing for my husband. In Jesus's name I pray, amen.

HERMAN

IT WAS ANTICIPATED that Jake would go home from the hospital two days following surgery, and that his transurethral catheter would remain in place for approximately ten days. This meant we needed to be trained in the care of the catheter and its bag. before he could be discharged

The nurse initially told us that I would have the responsibility of emptying the catheter bag. Her instruction immediately threw me back to my teenaged years when I'd helped care for my father. Following a serious injury at work, he had lain in a hospital bed in our living room. At that time, my job had been to empty the forty-eight-ounce can he used during the day as a urinal. I used to gag at that pungent smell and I gagged now as the memory surfaced. I wasn't sure I was up to the task of emptying Jake's catheter bag.

But I didn't share my recollection.

"Since Jake's attached to the catheter," I suggested instead, "maybe it would be better if he had the job of emptying the bag."

Both the nurse and Jake agreed to that plan. My job was to make certain the bag didn't get too full, even if it meant checking on it during the night.

It felt so good to have Jake home from the hospital. Without any worry on my part, he developed his own strategies to avoid pulling on the catheter tube when he stood.

A few days later, early one morning, he said, "I've decided to name my catheter bag."

"You have?" I asked, utterly surprised. Then I giggled. "I hadn't realized you'd grown so fond of the old bag."

Jake's reply was simple and to the point. "Yup. I've decided to call him Herman."

"Herman? Why Herman?"

The only Herman I knew was my biological mother's second husband, and he was someone I'd never warmed up to. Now Jake wanted to name his catheter bag Herman? *Weird*.

"Don't know," he said. "Just like the name, I suppose."

When I checked on the amount of urine in the catheter bag later that day, I affectionately referred to the bag by its new name.

"Let's see how Herman is doing!" I declared.

We both laughed.

A few days later, our children and grandchildren had gathered at our dining room table for our usual Sunday lunch. During a lull in the conversation, Jake matter-of-factly told them about the name.

This caught everyone's attention. Jake wasn't typically known for being creative, and besides, the announcement was perhaps a little absurd, especially at the lunch table.

"Herman." Our oldest daughter raised her eyebrow and cocked her head in disbelief.

Our son-in-law laughed. "Herman, huh?"

Our grandchildren all giggled.

But it was our youngest daughter's question that sent the adults into a fit of uproarious laughter. "Herman? As in Pee-wee Herman?"

The laughter intensified and raised questions from our grandchildren.

"Why is that so funny?"

"Who is Pee-wee Herman anyway?"

A few days later, I started a text conversation with our daughter in Alberta, telling her all about this intensely silly situation. Her responses were brief and polite. Unbeknownst to me, however, it turned out that Jake was texting her the story at exactly the same time.

When she eventually stopped responding to me, I asked her whether this was a good time to chat.

"Not really, mom," she texted. "I am currently sitting in a Bible study!"

In the midst of Jake's battle with this horrible disease, we cried many tears. But we also laughed a lot. Why? Because we knew that our happiness wasn't based on our circumstances. Rather, it was based on the solid foundation of Whose we were and what He had done for us. We understood it was a joy to be able to laugh and still rejoice in God our Saviour in the midst of life's struggles.

Meanwhile, Jake waited for the day the catheter would be removed.

> Though the fig tree does not bud and there are no grapes on the vines, though the olive crop fails and the fields produce no food, though there are no sheep in the pen and no cattle in the stalls, yet I will rejoice in the Lord, I will be joyful in God my Savior. (Habakkuk 3:17–18)

THE CYSTOGRAM

Be joyful in hope, patient in affliction, faithful in prayer.
(Romans 12:12)

IT WAS A beautiful day in April when we once again journeyed down our country roads to the hospital in the city. Spring was evident: the grass was turning green, birds were busy building nests, and the sun shone brightly.

"It won't be long now and planting will start," Jake declared, revealing his farmer's heart.

It was the tenth day following Jake's surgery and he was scheduled for a cystogram to measure the bladder's ability to expel urine. The catheter would then be removed as long as the bladder worked properly.

As he had already done on several occasions, when we arrived at the hospital lobby Jake took a number from the dispenser and then sat down to wait. When his number was called, he approached the registration desk.

Once again, rather than give the clerk his name, he smiled wide and gave her his birthday: "May 3, 1948."

The clerk didn't think it was funny—at all. I maintained my composure even though I was laughing hysterically inside my head. I honestly didn't recognize my husband; it was unlike him to be so humorous.

Must be a side effect from the anaesthetic, I thought.

The clerk took his full name, address, and then had him repeat his birthdate. She gave him directions towards another part of the hospital.

"When you get there," she said, "be certain to register again."

We followed the pathway until we arrived at the appropriate department. Since this waiting room was empty, Jake went directly to the registration desk and sat down. The clerk looked up and asked him for his number.

A little confused, he asked, "What number?"

The Waiting Room

The clerk appeared frustrated. She abruptly raised her arm and flapped her index finger to the location of the number dispenser on the wall, several feet behind him.

"Please take a number. Then have a seat in the waiting area."

Both Jake and Herman joined me in the empty waiting room. Our eyes met as he sat down. Without speaking a word, we slowly and simultaneously turned and looked behind us at all of the vacant chairs. With our eyebrows raised, we shrugged our shoulders and grinned at the absurdity of the situation.

Things became even more comical when, less than fifteen seconds after sitting down, the woman called Jake's number.

Jake and Herman returned to the registration desk, where he handed the number to the woman and once again introduced himself and stated that he was there for a cystogram.

She looked at the screens on her desk. "I don't see you here in my computer," she said curtly. "Are you sure it was for today?"

"Certain."

I wanted to say, "Look lady. He's not in your computer! He's sitting right here in front of you!" But I decided to keep my ridiculous humour to myself. She didn't seem to be in the mood for a chuckle.

"When's your birthday?" she asked.

Our laughter once again had to remain internal. By this point, I was having my own private party.

Jake also thought it was hysterical, but he didn't laugh. Instead he maintained his typical quiet and calm demeanour and replied politely and respectfully. "May 3, 1948."

I wanted to introduce her to Herman and tell her that his birthday was April 1, 2019, but I quickly held back the words in fear of setting this woman's frustrations over the edge. She was obviously having a bad day.

We watched while she slid her mouse around on its pad, clicked buttons, and looked from one computer screen to another. Finally she looked up and told Jake that his appointment was in two weeks.

Jake had no intention of having Herman hang around for another two weeks, because over time the catheter had become quite uncomfortable. He insisted that his appointment was not in two weeks, but rather right now.

The Cystogram

In hopes of adding clarity, I further explained that his surgery date had been moved up two weeks. It had therefore been our understanding that the date for the cystogram had been moved up as well.

The clerk returned to her computer screens, clearly flustered by the conflicting information. She then looked up at Jake and again asked—again—for his birthdate.

While she continued to search for him in her computer, I called the surgeon's office and explained the situation. I was reassured that Jake did have an immediate appointment for a cystogram. In turn, the surgeon's office called the clerk, who quite miraculously found Jake in her computer.

"They will see if they can fit you in today," she commented rather than apologize.

At that, she again directed us to take a seat in the still empty waiting room.

We sat.

We waited.

Jake's name was called. He squeezed my thigh as he rose to follow the voice.

I sat.

I waited for him.

Alone in an empty waiting room.

A young mother came into the waiting room with her two small children. I appreciated the distraction.

Before long, I heard Jake's gentle tenor voice calling my name. We followed the technician to another area of the hospital where he was directed to lay on a hospital bed.

"Someone will be with you shortly," the kind young lady said as she walked away.

We waited.

A very friendly nurse came over to check in on Jake. After confirming his name, she asked for his birthdate.

"The doctor will be with you shortly," she said.

As she stepped away, Jake turned to me. "Really? I really think I should just have my birthdate tattooed on my forehead!"

Our laughter broke the tension.

Before long, the doctor came and greeted us in his usual friendly and professional manner. He asked Jake a number of questions regarding how things had been since the surgery. Jake explained that he had no complaints other than feeling extremely tired and somewhat sore. The doctor checked the stitches, reported that the cystogram was clear, and added that the nurse would come in a few minutes to remove the catheter.

"I'll see you in about a month's time."

The nurse returned to remove the catheter.

"Take a deep breath while I count to three," she said.

Jake took a deep breath. From her instructions, he anticipated that the catheter would be removed once she said three. But when the nurse said two, she pulled firmly on the catheter tube. Out it came!

On our way home from the hospital, we stopped at our favourite ice cream shop for a Boston cooler. While we waited for our order, Jake suddenly turned to me.

"Text the kids and tell them," he said excitedly.

"Tell them what?"

"Tell them Pee-wee Herman has been laid to rest!"

> Prayer: Lord Jesus, we are so aware that happiness can brighten our day. But we are also aware that happiness is often based on those things happening around us. Help us, Lord, to always be joyful, to always rejoice in our hearts because of You, Father, in spite of our circumstances and in spite of our happenings. We continue to praise and thank You for all that You have done for us. In Jesus's name we pray, amen.

IN THE WAITING ROOM CALLED MOANS AND GROANS

IN THE GOSPELS, Jesus "often withdrew to lonely places and prayed" (Luke 5:16). Other times, He thanked the Father for food (Matthew 26:26–27). He even prayed to His Father while dying on the cross: "Father, forgive them, for they do not what they are doing" (Luke 23:34). In these ways, Jesus modelled for us the importance of prayer.

Jesus valued prayer so much that He took the time to teach us how to pray. In the Sermon on the Mount, He gave instructions: "when you pray, go into your room, close the door and pray to your Father, who is unseen" (Matthew 6:6).

Jesus then taught us the prayer that has become so very familiar:

> Our Father in heaven, hallowed be your name, your kingdom come, your will be done, on earth as it is in heaven. Give us today our daily bread. And forgive us our debts, as we also have forgiven our debtors. And lead us not into temptation, but deliver us from the evil one. (Matthew 6:9–13)

This prayer encourages us to praise God, seek His provision, ask for forgiveness, forgive others, and request protection from the enemy.

Jake valued those times when he talked to his heavenly Father. While in this place of waiting, Jake knew he could speak to Jesus at any time. Jake told me that he often prayed for his health to be restored. He also pleaded with the Lord to remove the cancer from his body.

But even though he believed, there were days when he felt physically and emotionally depleted. On those days, he found it difficult to stay focused in prayer. Discouragement grew fangs, sat beside him, and taunted him with persistent thoughts like Has the cancer spread? or If so, where to? or How much time do I have left? He tried hard to dispel these negative thoughts, but they could block him from praying.

I occasionally noticed a blank expression on Jake's face. My gut told me that he was worried and his thoughts in upheaval.

"What's on your mind?" I would ask him.

For the most part, he was unable to translate into words the turmoil he felt in his spirit. But his usual response was simple and familiar: "God's got it!"

Jake believed that the Lord knew what he was going through. He shared with me that this brought him great comfort.

> ...for your Father knows what you need before you ask him. (Matthew 6:8)

There had been other times in his life when he didn't know how to pray. Yet he was both comforted and astounded that Spirit Himself had interceded for him.

> In the same way, the Spirit helps us in our weakness. We do not know what we ought to pray for, but the Spirit himself intercedes for us through wordless groans. (Romans 8:26)

We imagined the Holy Spirit as He interceded for Jake before the Father. We imagined Him groaning with inexpressible words. It comforted us to know that if the Holy Spirit's utterances for Jake were wordless groans, it must also be okay for Jake to utter his prayers in this same way. Because, in essence, Jake's groans and moans were prayers.

It was my practice to wake early in the morning to pray.

> In the morning, Lord, you hear my voice; in the morning I lay my requests before you and wait expectantly. (Psalm 5:3)

Because Jake always rose earlier than I did, I made it a habit to pray for him when I went to bed in the evening. Night after night, I brought Jake before the Lord and asked for healing. While he slept, I wrapped my arms around him and laid my hand on his back approximately where I thought the prostate had been. I prayed. I asked the Lord to take the cancer away. I asked the Lord to heal him. I begged the Lord not to take my husband home.

One day we received an email from a friend who told us that she and her husband prayed for Jake every day. We felt so honoured that they would take their time and energy to remember Jake in prayer.

A few days later, when Jake and I were having a very low day, her husband called to see how we were doing and again mentioned that he and his wife prayed for us every day.

We were also aware that our children and siblings, not to mention many others, prayed for him on a daily and regular basis. We believed that Jesus heard each and every one of those prayers.

It became our practice to sit in this waiting room of prayer. We visited it frequently. While there, we prayed, cried, moaned, and groaned. We knew the Lord heard every word, whether spoken or unspoken.

We prayed.

We asked others to pray.

We prayed while we waited.

> Prayer: Dear Jesus, we thank You and praise You for hearing our moans and groans and interceding on our behalf. We thank You for nudging others to pray for Jake. Forgive us for those times when we find it difficult to trust You. Please protect us from becoming discouraged. In Jesus's name we pray, amen.

A MOMENT

In the morning, Lord, you hear my voice; in the morning I lay
my requests before you and wait expectantly. (Psalm 5:3)

ONCE A MAN has a prostatectomy, the PSA should drop to zero because there's no longer a prostate to produce the antigen. As a result, Jake had his blood monitored regularly. We held onto the hope that his PSA levels would go into freefall.

To prepare for his upcoming six-week follow-up appointment, Jake attended for bloodwork.

Then we waited, hoped, and prayed. We tried to be optimistic and hopeful. Some days that was easy, but most of the time the waiting felt painful. My mind would wander to the worst possible outcomes.

I attempted to distract myself by finding things that brought me beauty and joy. I reflected on the years we had been married, recognizing that there had always been food on the table and we'd never gone hungry. We'd always had clothes to wear. And of course we'd had our three most beautiful and precious daughters, and later on two wonderful sons-in-law and six grandchildren. We loved and enjoyed their personalities—and their questions.

I loved my husband and how handsome he looked when he was clean-shaven! I praised and thanked God for His continued provision for me and our family.

As I remembered all this, I realized that I hadn't been taking the time to appreciate the small things in life. That realization prompted me to stop.

Then I saw. The moments. They showed up at random times. They often came simply, and often surprisingly. Like the number 55555 on the odometer of our SUV. It was a reminder that we had travelled that many kilometres safely.

Another time, I was fascinated by a ladybug in our house, signifying the joy of another spring. I also recalled when we'd moved my broken-down sewing machine. This made me reminisce about the clothing it had sewed and mended over the forty-two years of our marriage.

The more often I took the time to appreciate the small things, the more I realized that these moments, when strung together, turned into hours, then days, then months, then years, then a lifetime.

It occurred to me that if I missed the moments, I might miss the life.

Early one morning, I felt compelled to get out of bed and look out our bedroom window. As I looked down to the gardens below, I longed to hear the chirping of birds. I imagined hearing the laughter of our children and grandchildren as they splashed and giggled in the pool.

At that, I was greeted with another moment: a glorious sunrise. I watched as the sun peeked over the top of the hip roof barn. Almost instantly, the beam of light spread out in hues of pink, gold, blue, and white as they greeted the world with the glory and hope of a new day.

I quickly grabbed my phone and snapped a couple of pictures in an effort to capture the moment so I could show Jake when he awoke. I returned to bed and applauded the Lord for the glorious beginning to my day.

"You missed it!" I told Jake when he stirred.

"Missed what?"

"The moment." My voice was a mixture of excitement and calm. "There was a moment this morning and you missed it. I tried to capture the sunrise for you."

I showed him my phone and Jake immediately got out of bed. He looked out the window and observed the sun, still painting the skies with a full palette of colours.

"Awwww, a moment," he prayerfully whispered.

> Prayer: Lord Jesus, we sit in awe of You, Creator of the universe. Thank You for the beauty of the world You have made and for giving it to us to enjoy, amen.

WATCH AND WAIT

> Yes, my soul, find rest in God; my hope comes from him.
> (Psalm 62:5)

SIX WEEKS FOLLOWING his prostatectomy, Jake attended his follow-up appointment. As he had done on many occasions before, Jake checked in at the front desk and we took a seat in the waiting room.

This time, however, the wait felt different.

Even though we already knew the cancer had spread outside the wall of the prostate and into the seminal vesicles, we still hoped for good news. We hoped that the pathology report would indicate that all the cancer had been removed and Jake could put this unfortunate experience with cancer behind him.

"Jacob Martens."

We stood together and followed the voice to the exam room.

As before, Dr. King knocked, entered, and greeted us in his friendly and welcoming manner.

He reviewed details about Jake's rising PSA, the initial findings from the biopsy, and the resulting need for surgery.

"The pathology report confirms what I already knew when I did the surgery," Dr. King said. "The cancer had broken outside the wall of the prostate. At the time of surgery, I did remove one lymph node and the pathology report shows that there was no cancer in that lymph node."

Both Jake and I sighed in relief.

"As I had already explained to you after the surgery, I also removed both seminal vesicles. And as I suspected, the pathology report shows that the cancer had indeed spread into that area as well. As a result of the information in this report, the pathologist has now upgraded the Gleason score from 7 to 8 and has deemed the cancer to be aggressive."

The Waiting Room

Aggressive? Now that was a horrible word!

The doctor calmly continued. "At this point in time, the recommendation is to watch and wait."

"Watch and wait for what?" I quickly asked.

Without a prostate, the doctor explained, Jake's most recent PSA result should have been zero. It still wasn't zero, although it was low.

"It can take a couple of months for the PSA to drop to zero following surgery," Dr. King said. "The body needs to catch up with the removal of the prostate."

He offered hope that the PSA could still drop further, and that the next three months would give us a better idea as to what our next steps should be.

"If the PSA drops to zero during that time, that's a good thing. It would indicate to us that we got all the cancer. But if it doesn't, if it still goes up, then we'll determine our next course of action, which most likely will be radiation. In the meantime, we watch and wait. We'll do more bloodwork in three months."

Even though we heard what the doctor told us, we felt such tension between the words aggressive and watch and wait. It felt like there should have been an immediate and more aggressive treatment available. Watch and wait didn't feel like any kind of treatment at all.

I chastised myself. After all, I wasn't a doctor, nor did I have any prior experience with prostate cancer. I knew I had to trust the doctor's recommendation.

Jake felt comfortable with this plan, but I felt rattled.

Once we got back to the car, I shared my frustrations.

"God's got it," he simply reminded me.

Little did we know then that watching and waiting would become a regular pattern of treatment over the course of this ongoing nightmare.

Watch and wait.

> Prayer: Lord Jesus, we are grateful that You've got it! You've got him! We wait for You while we watch to see how You will intervene in Jake's battle with cancer. But Lord, the waiting is so hard. I am so tired of waiting. In Jesus's name I pray, amen.

IN THE WAITING ROOM CALLED ANXIETY

> But as for me, I watch in hope for the Lord, I wait for God my Saviour; my God will hear me. (Micah 7:7)

WE HAD OFTEN talked about places we wanted to see and things we eventually wanted to do, but when we had the desire and the energy to do something we often didn't have the time or money. Then, when we had the money and energy, we didn't have the time.

With Jake's declining health, we recognized that we had arrived at an interesting point in our lives where we had the time and the money, but no longer the necessary energy.

When I arrived home from work one day, Jake wasn't in the house. I assumed he was in his garden, so I headed outside in hopes that I would find him there.

Jake loved his garden. He took great pride in planting and caring for the crops of sweet corn, strawberries, green beans, tomatoes, and radishes. He kept the garden organized, fertilized, and weed-free. He enjoyed the challenge of growing giant pumpkins, one of which had once won a red ribbon at our local agricultural fair for being the largest pumpkin.

But when I stepped into his garden on this particular day, my heart sank. It was so apparent that Jake no longer had the energy to maintain it, at least to his usual standard. A large part of the garden was covered in weeds. In addition, some of the plants had grown wild and choked out smaller and weaker ones.

When we connected in the barn a few minutes later, I lovingly said to him, "I was in the garden. What's going on?"

He sighed deeply, then shrugged his shoulders and slumped in an almost defeated posture. "I can't keep up."

"Is it time to downsize?"

The Waiting Room

He quickly responded with relief in his voice. "I was thinking the same thing!"

As we talked about downsizing the garden, we also considered whether it was time to downsize our house and our yard. Without hesitation, we listed our property for sale and looked for a new home with a yard that was much smaller than four acres.

We cleaned and packed, deciding what to keep, what to give away, and what to toss in the garbage. We asked ourselves whether every item we wanted to keep was something we needed or something we wanted because of the sentimental value we had attached to it.

Jake also focused his energy on cleaning out the barns. While doing so, he came across many items which had been saved over the generations just in case they were needed again.

Occasionally, he uncovered an object that stirred a childhood memory.

"I remember this!" he said to me one day when I was with him in the barn. "My grandparents used this to shell corn."

He held up an obsolete device no longer needed due to newer farming practices and equipment.

Before we knew it, three months had passed. The time had come for Jake's next blood test. Two days later, he went online to obtain the results.

His PSA was still elevated, an indication that the cancer was still present in his body. We were very disappointed. We had both prayed. Others had prayed.

At first, we came to terms with the news and believed the doctor would have a plan for treatment. But the two-week gap between receiving the results and seeing his doctor gave us too much time and opportunity to think. It gave us a chance to wonder how bad this news really was. This triggered our worry and fear, which in turn triggered even more worry and fear. Before we knew it, our thoughts and feelings were spiralling out of control. We found ourselves worrying about the worst case scenarios. Disappointment, defeat, and discouragement combined forces, stomped on hope, and invited fear to join their party.

All of this put us in a waiting room called anxiety, where fear and worry lurked in every corner. We got stuck here, believing that because something felt bad, it must be bad.

We had forgotten about faith. Like old relics found in the barn, their purposes and value long forgotten, we had forgotten about the many occasions in our lives when we had experienced God's faithfulness.

So we talked while we worked and reminisced about those many times when God had been so trustworthy. As we remembered, we renewed the values and purposes of the lessons we'd learned. This helped us to refocus on Him, our faith in Him, and His faithfulness.

We remembered.

While we waited.

> Prayer: Lord Jesus, we confess that sometimes disappointment, defeat, and discouragement take over our thoughts and we forget about the faith we have in You as our loving God who died for us. Help us to remember those many times in our lives when You have been so trustworthy. Help us to focus our thoughts on You and Your faithfulness to us. In Jesus's name we pray, amen.

IN THE WAITING ROOM CALLED TRUST

Therefore I tell you, do not worry about your life, what you will eat or drink; or about your body, what you will wear. Is not life more than food, and the body more than clothes? Look at the birds of the air; they do not sow or reap or store away in barns, and yet your heavenly Father feeds them. Are you not much more valuable than they? Can any one of you by worrying add a single hour to your life? (Matthew 6:25–27)

MANY YEARS PRIOR to Jake's diagnosis, in approximately the third year of our marriage, we found ourselves in a difficult financial situation. We were expecting our second child, our summer crops hadn't done well, and we had many bills to pay. In addition, the economy wasn't good, interest rates were extremely high, and Jake had been unable to find work for the winter.

In order to alleviate the pressure, Jake tried to sell some used equipment by placing an advertisement in a farmers' newspaper. Unfortunately, we didn't receive any interest. This left us feeling discouraged because there seemed to be no solution to our financial strain.

We prayed many times. We didn't know which way to turn.

Several months later, on a cold day in January, Jake decided that it was time to take out a loan for $2,000 to carry us financially until the spring. This was 1980 and $2,000 would be approximately $8,000 in 2024.

Shortly after he left to go to the bank, he came back into the house and threw $2,000 in cash on the kitchen table. I was very confused because I couldn't understand how he had gotten into town, spoken to our banker, and found his way home again in such a short period of time. I also wondered why he had brought the money home with him.

"Why didn't you put the money in our bank account?" I asked.

Jake was very excited. "Listen to what just happened!"

He shared with me that when he'd left to go to the bank, a man had been standing by the barn looking at the silo. When Jake approached, the man shared that he was responding to the ad Jake had posted in the newspaper the previous September.

After examining the silo, he offered Jake $1,800.

Jake explained that he was just on his way to the bank to borrow $2,000 so he could feed his family and pay his bills for the rest of the winter.

Without hesitating, the man reached into his pocket, paid Jake the full amount, in cash, and then added, "I'll be back in May to pick up the silo."

We always believed that this had been God's intervention in our lives. Perhaps a miracle. The gentleman had paid the exact amount Jake needed, paying for it on a cold winter day in January in response to an ad posted the previous September.

Our trust in God had been clearly established. This experience had encouraged us many times in our marriage to believe in our God, who always provided our needs. Because we had experienced His faithfulness to us then, and many times since, we knew He was trustworthy.

But perhaps due to our human nature, we sometimes forgot about God's faithfulness and have to learn to trust again. While we wait.

> Prayer: Lord Jesus, we praise You for the many times we have experienced Your intervention in our lives. Thank You for always providing for our needs. Forgive us for forgetting. Please help us to remember, Lord. We once again commit Jake's health into Your loving care and ask for a miracle, Lord. We ask for him to be completely healed. In Jesus's name we pray, amen.

GOD'S GOT IT!

> Because of the Lord's great love we are not consumed, for his compassions never fail. They are new every morning; great is your faithfulness. I say to myself, "The Lord is my portion; therefore I will wait for him. (Lamentations 3:22–24)

ONE DAY JAKE said to me, "Trusting God is a lesson I've had to learn over and over. Many things have happened in my life where I had to learn to trust God. Then, just as I thought I had the trust thing all figured out, I had to learn that lesson all over again. It's all about trust, trust, trust!"

He reminisced about an experience he'd had many years prior. He had found himself standing in a tomato field following a heavy rainfall. His rubber boots were stuck in the mud and water almost flowed over their tops. He felt so helpless as he watched the once healthy plants wither in the hot summer sun. He desperately tried to drain the water off the field, but his efforts were in vain. He was very emotional when he came back into the house that day, feeling so defeated that he had cried.

"I didn't know which way to turn," he recalled. "We invested so much money in that crop and it was all being washed away. Literally! But looking back on that experience, I knew all that I had to do was draw on my faith in God. That gave me the strength to move forward."

His former experiences with learning to trust God helped him through his battle with cancer. Most days, he had the unwavering ability to trust God, no matter what. It was an expectant mindset. Jake trusted God. Repeatedly.

But he admitted that sometimes he struggled to remain in that headspace. On those days, his trust in God wavered, especially when the struggles stared him right in the eyes.

It was difficult to trust God while he waited. These periods caused him to vacillate between his belief and unbelief. Some days he questioned whether God was still there and whether God really had his best interests in mind. Other days, he spoke to God and told Him that he struggled with the reasons that this disease had entered his body.

"Why?" he asked God.

Doubt grew and invited its cousins, worry and fear, to band together. Like nasty weeds in a garden, they attempted to choke out trust. This heightened Jake's anxiety about his health, life, and future.

When I noticed that Jake appeared low in his affect, I took it as an opportunity to remind him of all the times he had repeatedly reminded me, "God's got it!"

That's when Jake once again invited the Lord to sit with him in the waiting room. To sit with him in his fear and pain. To sit with him in his doubt and discouragement.

When he invited Jesus to join him in the waiting, His presence empowered Jake to open the door and tell fear, worry, and doubt to leave. Then he again moved to the waiting room of trust and focused on Jesus.

"It's all about trust, trust, trust—in Him!" Jake would say… not once, not twice, but three times. "God's got it!"

> Prayer: Lord Jesus, there are days when the enemy tries to convince us to doubt You. Forgive us for believing him. Forgive us for doubting You. We know that You've got it! In Jesus's name we pray, amen.

WAITING ON THE CREATOR

> Lord, our Lord, how majestic is your name in all the earth! You have set your glory in the heavens... When I consider your heavens, the work of your fingers, the moon and the stars, which you have set in place... (Psalm 8:1, 3)

LATE ONE FALL night, Jake was totally awestruck by God, Creator of the universe. He had been at the back of the farm with his tractor and wagons waiting for his brother to finish combining a field of soybeans. For whatever reason, Jake felt compelled to shut off the tractor and sit for a moment in the quiet. Before he knew it, he found himself lying on the ground as he stared up into the clear, bright night sky. Breathless, he gazed upon the absolute splendour of countless stars, planets, and a full moon as they illuminated the heavens, in awe of God who had not only created the universe but was aware of every detail in it.

He recalled Psalm 147:4—"He determines the number of the stars and calls them each by name"—and felt humbled, realizing that he was just a small speck beneath that night sky. Yet just like the stars, he was fully aware that because he too had been created by God, God knew him by name as well. In fact, God knew all about him and cared for him.

> ...what is mankind that you are mindful of them, human beings that you care for them? You made them a little lower than the angels and crowned them with glory and honour. (Psalm 8:4–5)

Jake knew that because God cared for him, He also knew what exactly his needs were.

Are not two sparrows sold for a penny? Yet not one of them will fall to the ground outside your Father's care. And even the very hairs of your head are all numbered. So don't be afraid; you are worth more than many sparrows. (Matthew 10:29–31)

Jake realized that he loved this amazing God who loved and valued him.

"This experience encouraged me to lean more on my faith," he later shared with me. "Going forward from there, I knew there was nothing I couldn't overcome, because I knew that my heavenly Father had His best in mind for me. While I waited."

RADIATION TREATMENTS

ON A PICTURESQUE August morning, we headed into the city for Jake's appointment to see the urologist. The fields boasted of an abundant upcoming harvest as soybeans matured, corn stalks stretched skyward, and pumpkins dotted the fields in shades of orange. From our perspective, living in the country couldn't compare with living anywhere else in the world.

That day, Dr. King shared his concern with us that Jake's PSA had increased. He too had been hoping it would drop to zero, but based on the latest information he strongly recommended that Jake begin radiation treatments.

An appointment was arranged for him to see the same oncologist he had seen approximately nine months earlier.

At that appointment two weeks later, the oncologist told us that he had reviewed Jake's pathology report and specifically made note of the elevated PSA.

He leaned back in his chair and looked directly at Jake. "I'm not sure what to tell you, Mr. Martens."

We were troubled to hear him start with such a statement. My first thought was that if he wasn't sure, how could he expect us to have any confidence in what he had to say next?

"By this point in time, the cancer has either stayed put in the prostate area or it has left the prostate area and travelled to somewhere else in your body." He paused. "Or, it has stayed in the prostate area and has also spread to somewhere else in your body."

Although we understood what he meant, we weren't comforted by those words.

The oncologist further explained that because he didn't know where the cancer may have spread, he felt it was best to focus the radiation in the area where the prostate had been.

The Waiting Room

Confidently he recommended thirty-three rounds of radiation. We swallowed hard.

Two and a half weeks later, we held hands as our synchronized steps once again carried us through the double doors of the cancer centre for Jake's first radiation treatment. A very pleasant and friendly greeter directed us to a desk where Jake registered, including his name and birthdate. We were then directed to a waiting room where Jake registered again.

From yet a third waiting room, near the radiation treatment rooms. Jake was called in. I was directed to take a seat in still another waiting room. His radiation treatment took less than half an hour, so my wait this time was brief.

Most of the time, I sat alone. These were good opportunities to just sit and rest my mind, body, and spirit. To rest assured in Him.

Early each morning over the course of the next seven weeks, except weekends and holidays, Jake and I made the nearly one-hour journey to the cancer centre. We enjoyed the sunrise, open fields, and eventual abundant harvest. Half an hour later, we would travel back home.

At first the radiation treatments didn't seem to have any effect on Jake, but as the treatments progressed he became more tired and slept for a couple of hours most afternoons.

I found it difficult to see this physically strong man sleep so much. From as far back as I could remember, Jake had worked hard and got physically exhausted. But no matter how tired he felt, a renewed energy surfaced in him whenever he heard the rhythmic whirr of his riding lawnmower or the buzz when he throttled the trigger of his chainsaw. Although it wasn't tangible and couldn't be seen, I would watch these sounds release his tension and renew his energy. It was always enough for him to complete the next task at hand.

It saddened me to watch him battle through prostate cancer and grow increasingly tired. I often wished his energy could be renewed as simply as hearing the hum from his lawnmower.

One day I was encouraged by a passage from Isaiah. It spoke of a God who never tires. He is a God who "gives strength to the weary and increases the power of the weak." I realized that when we put our hope in Him, our renewal may not necessarily be a physical one; it could be an emotional and spiritual renewal. When we put our hope in Him, that's when He renews our strength.

> Do you not know? Have you not heard? The Lord is the everlasting God, the Creator of the ends of the earth. He will not grow tired or weary, and his understanding no one can fathom. He gives strength to the weary and increases the power of the weak. Even youths grow tired and weary, and young men stumble and fall; but those who hope in the Lord will renew their strength. They will soar on wings like eagles; they will run and not grow weary, they will walk and not be faint. (Isaiah 40:28–31)

We hoped and prayed that the radiation treatments would be effective in killing any residual cancer.

We hoped and prayed.

While we waited.

FAITH, HOPE, AND LOVE

And now these three remain: faith, hope and love. But the greatest of these is love. (1 Corinthians 13:13)

WHILE ON OUR honeymoon in Bermuda, we were required to dress formally for supper. I'll always remember walking hand in hand down the corridor of the hotel as we headed to the dining room. Jake wore his grey three-piece pinstriped suit and I wore a black dress. Eight inches taller than me, I felt secure in his shadow, assured of his love, and so blessed and proud to have him as my husband.

Since then, we have been through many ups and downs. Our marriage hasn't been perfect, because neither of us were perfect. Over the years, we struggled through difficult seasons, but we got through those times because of our faith, and because of the love we had for each other.

Dr. King had warned us that along with the normal risks of surgery, there was the possibility of long-term complications directly related to the removal of the prostate. The most common of these complications included urinary incontinence and erectile dysfunction.

In their book, Prostate Cancer, Drs. Fred Saad and Michael McCormack note:

> About 50 percent of men who undergo a radical prostatectomy [complete removal of the prostate] will develop permanent erectile dysfunction.[3]
>
> Approximately 1 to 5 percent of men who have had a radical prostatectomy experience total and permanent urinary incontinence.[4]

---

[3] Saad, Fred and Michael McCormack, *Prostate Cancer: Understanding the Disease and Its Treatment, Fourth Edition* (Montral, QC: Annika Parance, 2015), 143.

[4] Ibid., 98.

Despite being profoundly impacted by both of these surgical complications, over time Jake adjusted. We also adjusted as a couple while we grieved the losses which resulted from those complications. Although it was difficult, we recognized that Jake's value as a man and the qualities he possessed hadn't changed.

In this continuing battle against prostate cancer, Jake recognized that his value lay in who he was in Christ Jesus, and that he was "fearfully and wonderfully made" (Psalm 139:14) and "God's handiwork, created in Christ Jesus to do good works, which God prepared in advance" for him to do" (Ephesians 2:10).

He also realized that, according to God's Word, he was honoured by God and had God-given responsibilities:

> …what is mankind that you are mindful of them, human beings that you care for them? You have made them a little lower than the angels and crowned them with glory and honor. You made them rulers over the works of your hands; you put everything under their feet: all flocks and herds, and the animals of the wild, the birds in the sky, and the fish in the sea, all that swim the paths of the seas.
> (Psalm 8:4–8)

He also possessed certain qualities that defined him as a man, as outlined by the apostle Paul: "righteousness, godliness, faith, love, endurance and gentleness" (1 Timothy 6:11).

Over the years, we have developed a friendship, a close bond and deep emotional intimacy, all of which were extremely valuable to us. More than four decades after our honeymoon, we continued to walk hand in hand, me still safe in his shadow and secure in his love. We leaned on our faith, confidently looked forward with hope, and rest assured of each other's love, a love that we knew would uphold us in this continuing battle with prostate cancer.

IN THE WAITING ROOM CALLED DISTRACTION

WHEN WE SOLD our property, our youngest daughter temporarily moved in with us because she had recently returned to school. We enjoyed her company, as well as the company of her dog, Archer.

Archer was a black lab-border collie mix but looked more like a border collie with his long nose and the white star-shaped patch of fur on his chest. He was a handsome dog who weighed in at eighty pounds. Archer loved to be outdoors. In the spring, he enjoyed standing in the rain, and in the winter months he bounced and frolicked through the fluffy flakes when it snowed. At bedtime, he reluctantly came inside to sleep.

Archer was well-trained. He came when he was called, sat when he was told to sit, and even shook a paw. It didn't take us long to discover that his favourite treat was pizza crust. Whenever we brought home a pizza, he ran wild from one door to the other, barking and crying while he begged for a bite or two.

His love for pizza crust was so outrageous that when our daughter asked him, "Would you like a piece of pizza crust?" he immediately laid down and posed like a majestic lion on an Egyptian pyramid. With his paws straight out in front of him, he held his head high with his jaw level to the floor.

When our daughter gave the command "Look at me!" Archer looked straight into her eyes while she placed a piece of pizza crust on each of his front paws. The entire time, he maintained his majestic posture and didn't move a muscle.

In order to keep his attention, she would cue him again: "Look at me!"

He never looked down at the treat sitting on his paws. Rather, he waited while he kept his eyes focused on her.

Only when he heard her say "Okay" did he take his eyes off her and eat his treat.

It amazed us to watch their interaction. But what amazed us the most was how he kept his eyes focused on her, focused on his master.

We were reminded of the account in Matthew of the fear Jesus's disciples felt when their boat was tossed about by a windstorm. When the disciples saw Jesus walk toward them on the water, they were afraid because they thought He was a ghost.

> "Lord, if it's you," Peter replied, "tell me to come to you on the water."
>
> "Come," he said.
>
> Then Peter got down out of the boat, walked on the water and came toward Jesus. But when he saw the wind, he was afraid and, beginning to sink, cried out, "Lord, save me!"
>
> Immediately Jesus reached out his hand and caught him. "You of little faith," he said, "why did you doubt?" (Matthew 14:29–31)

When Peter saw the wind, he was afraid. More specifically, when he looked at the wind, he took his eyes off Jesus. When Peter was distracted by the storm, he took his eyes off the Master.

We recognized that we, too, had been distracted by the storm and taken our eyes off the Master. We knew that we needed to keep our eyes on the Lord!

On the One who had created Jake and made him "fearfully and wonderfully" (Psalm 139:14).

On the One who had formed him in his mother's womb (Psalm 139:13).

On the One who had not forgotten about him: "Are not five sparrows sold for two pennies? Yet not one of them is forgotten by God. Indeed, the very hairs of your head are all numbered. Don't be afraid; you are worth more than many sparrows" (Luke 12:6–7).

On the One who had sacrificed His life for him, for me, for us: "He sacrificed for their sins once for all when he offered himself" (Hebrews 7:27).

Prayer: Lord, while we continue to wait, please help us to keep our eyes focused on You rather than on the storms of life. Thank You for being our Creator, giver, and sustainer of life. In Jesus's name we pray, amen.

IN THE WAITING ROOM CALLED FAITH

IN HIS FIRST letter to the Corinthians, Paul refers to the gift of faith, writing, "to another faith by the same Spirit" (1 Corinthians 12:9). In this passage, the Greek word for faith is pistis, meaning "to be firmly persuaded as to something, and to believe with the idea of hope and certain expectation."[5]

In the book of James, we read,

> Be patient, then, brothers and sisters, until the Lord's coming. See how the farmer waits for the land to yield its valuable crop, patiently waiting for the autumn and spring rains. You too, be patient and stand firm, because the Lord's coming is near. (James 5:7–8)

In this passage, the Greek root word for wait is ekdechomai, which means "to await; expect and look for."[6] Ekdechomai's synonym is anameno, meaning "to wait for in confident expectancy."[7]

Many have told us that they've seen the gift of faith at work in Jake's life. I too have repeatedly seen that quiet and confident faith at work in him; although he doesn't have a strong ability to verbalize it, he has always exemplified his faith through his confident expectation in the Lord.

This was so apparent that after he eagerly worked up his farmland every spring, planting a variety of seeds, usually corn and soybeans, he would consistently worry and question his abilities, asking himself questions like "Did I work up the land properly?" or "Did I plant under the most ideal conditions?" or "Did I plant the seeds deep enough into the moisture?"

---

[5] *Hebrew-Greek Key Word Study Bible* (Chattanooga, TN: AMG Publishers, 2008), 2253.

[6] Ibid., 1538.

[7] Ibid.

Almost immediately, that worry would turn into prayer. I once heard him pray, "Lord, I really could use some rain." Then, in the early morning hours when the rain gently fell, I'd hear him praise God in a gentle whisper: "Thank You, Lord!"

Then he would wait.

But while he waited for the seeds to grow, Jake followed a most intriguing ritual. Every day, he walked out to the field and brushed the dirt away from a few seeds to see whether they had sprouted. I didn't understand his need to do that, and I often challenged him as having a lack of faith in his ability and in God. I even said things to him like "Oh, leave the field alone! God will let it grow." Other times, I said, "Honestly, if you keep stirring up the seeds, there won't be a crop left when it does decide to grow!"

One day, my husband tapped me on the shoulder and asked me to join him in his daily excursion to check the fields. Once we arrived at the edge of the field, he bent down and brushed the dirt away from one of the seeds to see whether it had sprouted. As he did, he said to me, "I like watching things grow."

We stepped a little farther into the field and he once again brushed the dirt away from another seed.

"Even though I know these seeds are now at God's mercy, it eases my mind to know that I did my best to give them the right start," he said.

We then knelt beside a third seed, and again he brushed the dirt away. This time he gently lifted the seed out of the ground and held it in his hand.

"The seed has sprouted!" he excitedly declared.

He lifted his hand and showed me the tiny plant growing out of the seed. He placed it into my hand.

"See? We get to feed the hungry!"

While I inspected the seed, I understood why he was exhilarated; it was an amazing feeling to hold that sprouted seed.

That was when it occurred to me that it wasn't my husband's lack of faith that led him to inspect the seeds each day. It was because of his faith!

We have inspected the fields together on many occasions. Patiently we wait with great expectation for the planted seeds to bring new life, food for the hungry, and provision for us. When there's no rain, or when we have unwanted pests or other diseases, we have done our best to remain strong and put our faith in Him as the giver of life.

Jake based his battle with cancer on the same faith, his hope and great expectation in a God who takes care of him.

So whenever Jake says "God's got it!" he really means that he is firmly persuaded with hope and certain expectation because He trusts Jesus.

He has put his faith in Him.

We put our faith in Him.

We continued to wait with confident and certain expectancy.

> Prayer: Lord Jesus, we know You are a faithful God. Help us, Lord, to wait with confidence while we expect Your intervention in Jake's health. In Jesus's name we pray, amen.

WAITING IN THE HALLWAY

> Do not be afraid. Stand firm and you will see the deliverance the Lord will bring you today... The Lord will fight for you; you need only to be still. (Exodus 14:13–14)

> Your enemy the devil prowls around like a roaring lion looking for someone to devour. (1 Peter 5:8)

A FEW MONTHS following his last radiation treatment, Jake complained of an unusual pain in his chest.

"I haven't felt well all day," he said to me when I arrived home from work. "I've had this pressure in my chest that won't go away, and this pain that goes down my arm."

He pointed to his left arm as he spoke.

We immediately went to the emergency room. Once he was triaged, he had an electrocardiogram (EKG) to assess the electrical activity of his heart. The doctor told Jake that the EKG didn't show a problem with his heart. There was no indication of a heart attack or irregular heartbeat.

Given Jake's symptoms, however, the doctor felt that a cardiac stress test was warranted. He referred Jake to a cardiac clinic.

Within a couple of days, Jake had appointments with the cardiologist for an ultrasound of his heart and for a cardiac stress test.

My phone rang just as we pulled into the parking lot of the cardiologist's office on the day of those tests. It was our real estate agent informing us that he had received a cash offer for our property, albeit considerably lower than our asking price. We thanked the agent for the phone call, turned down the offer, and then made our way into the cardiologist's office.

After Jake registered at the front desk, we were directed to have a seat in the waiting room.

The Waiting Room

"Jacob Martens."

Together we rose and followed the voice.

A nurse took Jake's medical history before directing us to another waiting room. There we watched a video that explained everything we would need to know about the stress test, how it was conducted, what to expect, and what to do and what not to do.

When the video was finished, we were led to the ultrasound room. Wires were attached to Jake's chest; these were used to monitor his heartrate and pulse. He was then directed to walk on a treadmill while the technician periodically increased the treadmill's speed and height. This was all in an effort to put stress on his heart.

Upon the doctor's cue, Jake was required to quickly step off the treadmill and lie down on a bed, at which time the doctor immediately did an ultrasound of his pulsating heart.

Meanwhile, I had been directed to stand in a specific spot where I had a full view of the heart monitor and ultrasounds. It was fascinating to watch Jake's thumping heart.

Jake was asked to return to the treadmill a second time. However, shortly after Jake started walking, the doctor abruptly stopped the procedure, directed Jake to get dressed, and asked us to meet him in his office.

Once we were in his office, the doctor instructed me to immediately take Jake to the emergency room. There appeared to be two blockages in Jake's heart.

"The hospital will prepare Jake for an angiogram," the doctor said.

I almost fell off my chair. Jake's jaw dropped open. He was shocked by this news, but it also triggered a memory of his father, who had died suddenly from a massive heart attack at the age of forty-nine.

As we drove to the hospital, Jake said, "We should be home in time for me to go bowling tonight, right?"

Oh, how I loved him. The simple and uncomplicated pleasures of life had always been important to him. Even in the middle of a crisis, he was thinking about his bowling team.

"Did you hear anything the doctor said?" I knew he had heard the doctor, but apparently he hadn't processed it.

"No. Not really."

Waiting In the Hallway

I explained to him why the doctor had wanted me to take him to the hospital. He was bewildered and then changed his question.

"So what do you think?" he asked. "Do you think I need to call Ed and let him know that I won't be able to go bowling tonight?"

My reply was calm and simple as I nodded my head. "I think that would be a good idea."

We entered through the emergency room doors of the hospital and registered at the front desk.

"Have a seat in the waiting room and someone will call you," we were told.

We complied.

We sat.

We waited.

In an effort to distract himself from the busyness of this downtown city hospital, Jake picked up a newspaper and started to read.

I, on the other hand, observed those around me. Some were stretched out on the floor. Others were obviously in pain. One young woman ran into the washroom to vomit. Some people were alone. Many were dirty, unkempt and appeared to be homeless.

"Jacob Martens!"

Together we followed the voice.

We were led down a long corridor at the back of the emergency department. Many people were lying on cots and emergency personnel waited with others who had arrived by ambulance.

A very kind nurse took a brief history from Jake and then hooked him up to a machine that monitored his blood pressure, heartrate, and pulse.

That hallway became our waiting room for the next several hours.

Despite the chaos around us, we both grew quiet while we listened to the low rumble of voices and moans.

When Jake eventually fell asleep, I took that as my opportunity to take a break. I headed down the hallway and found a washroom. Although it was marked "patients only," there appeared to be no patients waiting to use the facility, so I ventured inside.

As soon as the door slammed shut behind me, I lost it.

The Waiting Room

The purging of my emotions came instantly and almost radically. I screamed and pulled on my hair. It was as if I had suddenly realized I was in the middle of a battle, albeit a spiritual one.

"Enough," I yelled. "Enough! You cannot have my husband, you cannot have our dignity, you cannot have it all!"

For whatever reason, I was suddenly reminded of the spiritual warfare I had battled many years earlier and recalled my pastor telling me: "Do not talk to the demons!"

I quickly changed direction and placed my attention on the Lord. I called out to Him.

"Lord, I know You are in control. I know that You stepped on the head of the serpent and won victory over him. Lord, I ask for Your protection now over Jake, over his heart, and over however long we will be in this hospital. I ask for your protection over us. I know that You are our protector and I ask for that right now. So much has gone on in the past year with Jake being diagnosed with cancer, with trying to sell our house, and now with his heart!"

By this point in time, I was stooped over with my elbows on my knees and both hands on my head while I pulled my hair.

"I'm not sure how much more he can take. I'm not sure how much more I can take! So I commit it all to You, Lord. In Jesus's mighty name I pray, amen."

I was calm when I opened the washroom door. There was so much noise in the hallway that I knew no one had heard my outcry—that is, no one except the Lord.

When I returned to Jake's side, I saw two of our girls with their father. Their beautiful faces, smiles, and love warmed my heart. I could almost hear God say to me, "I love you."

Within a few minutes, Jake's cot was wheeled into an exam room. A nurse took a recent history, followed by another nurse who introduced herself as a student and then asked for permission to also take a recent medical history. Jake readily provided her with the information she requested.

Just as she stepped away, my cell phone rang. It was our real estate agent letting us know that the potential purchasers had agreed to increase their offer to meet our asking price.

After six months of waiting and after sixty-eight showings, our property had finally sold!

While lying on a hospital bed in emergency, Jake and I e-signed an agreement of purchase and sale to sell the property Jake had lived in since the day he was born.

A doctor then took a brief history, examined Jake, and told him that he would be admitted to the urgent care wing of the hospital and be scheduled for an angiogram on the following day.

We prayed.

Others prayed.

The next day, our eldest daughter sat with me while the doctor did the angiogram. Once completed, we were asked to join the doctor at Jake's bedside, at which time he told us that Jake's arteries were "pristine." Perfectly clear.

"You might want to have your stomach investigated," the doctor said. "There are times when stomach acid can mimic the pain and sensations you've described."

Jake and I looked at each other in wonder. Had the arteries been pristine when he was at the cardiologist's office for the stress test? It didn't sound like it. Was it possible that he had been healed in the interim?

We left the hospital the next day knowing that we would likely never know the answer to those questions.

A few days later, Jake had an appointment to see an internist with a view to having a scope of his stomach.

But—

—along came COVID.

> Prayer: Lord Jesus, thank You so much for fighting for us, for Jake! We are so grateful that our property sold, and for his pristine arteries! Thank You! We are also so aware that "the devil prowls around like a roaring lion looking for someone to devour" (1 Peter 5:8). Please protect us. In Jesus's name we pray, amen.

WAITING IN MY CAR

JAKE AND I quietly stared in disbelief at our television. The rapidly spreading coronavirus identified as COVID-19 had caused the once bustling city of Wuhan, China to shut down, leaving it motionless.

By the end of January 2020, the World Health Organization (WHO) declared the virus an international concern but had not yet called it a pandemic.

In the middle of March 2020, I received a telephone call instructing me to shut down our walk-in counselling clinic at the hospital due to the virus.

"Finish out the day and then go home," my supervisor said. "I'll get back to you."

Her direction was firm. I heard the angst in her voice.

When I questioned her further, I was met with an emphatic response: "We have no choice. The hospital has instructed us to do so."

A week later, Canada's prime minister, Justin Trudeau, spoke resolutely to the Canadian people. "Enough is enough. Go home and stay home!" He pleaded for Canadians abroad to return as soon as possible, no matter where they were in the world. Then he continued: "And if you are home, stay home!"

Dr. Theresa Tam, the Chief Medical Officer for Canada, stood near the prime minister during his address. In our opinions, their faces looked worried.

Before long, the virus appeared to travel eastward across the country, and eventually Ontario was shut down. Students stayed home from school and businesses and some stores were closed. People were in a frenzy as they stocked up on food and other household items, including toilet paper.

COVID-19 impacted how our world functioned. Plexiglass barriers went up in grocery stores and businesses. Fast food became accessible only by drive-thru. Wearing face masks became the norm, and in many instances were considered mandatory. It felt like our world had been turned upside-down. This became evident to me when I entered the bank one day and noticed a sign posted on the front door: "Masks must be worn before entering."

Oh my, I thought. *It used to be that they'd call the police if you entered the bank wearing a mask! What in the world has happened?*

Even though the medical professionals were doing their best in the ever-changing environment, there was still an impact on healthcare, in particular as it related to Jake's appointments. Even though he had previously been referred for a scope of his stomach, this procedure was delayed due to a backlog in medical tests and surgeries.

Many medical appointments also changed. Those that had been in-person appointments with the doctor became appointments by telephone or video conference.

Naturally, medical tests at the hospital required him to be physically present. But it meant he wasn't allowed a support person to go with him. Booking clerks simply told me to drop him off at the front door. He would call when he was finished.

While adjusting to these changes, Jake needed to attend the hospital for an ultrasound. As we'd been instructed, I dropped him off at the front door and prayed as he walked away from the vehicle.

An empty and hollow feeling overpowered me. I waited until I couldn't see him anymore and then quietly said "Bye."

On that day, rather than park at the hospital, I decided to park a few blocks away in a church parking lot, the same church where I'd been baptized as a seventeen-year-old. Although I knew I could pray anywhere at any time, this felt like the perfect place to pray and be calm before the Lord.

But when I arrived at the church, the entrance was barricaded. I surmised that it was most likely to prevent people, like me, from parking there rather than at the hospital.

I decided to park at the building next door, a pub. Since it was early in the morning, I guessed that it was closed, even though there were two cars in the parking lot.

As soon as I parked, I was immediately flooded with emotions. Sadness, fear, anger, and confusion all came to the surface. I crumbled under the emotional weight, broke down, and wept like a baby. I knew that these emotions were normal and that it was okay to take the time to feel them. It actually felt good to cry.

When I had slightly pulled myself together, I noticed two men exiting the pub. I speculated that they had been cleaning. But then I thought, *Maybe they spent the night there because they were too inebriated to drive home.*

As I pondered this, I noticed them looking at me. They pointed towards my car, faced each other, then again pointed in my direction. What were they saying about me? After all, when I looked in my rearview mirror I saw that my eyes were swollen and mascara ran down my cheeks. I was not a pretty sight.

Then it struck me that it was possible they were having the same thoughts about me I had just had about them: Poor old soul. She probably had too much to drink last night and ended up sleeping it off in her car!

Of course, I had no idea what they were thinking. But in my self-imposed embarrassment over someone mistaking me for a drunk, I started the car and headed back to the hospital. Ironically, when I arrived I learned that parking was free that day!

When Jake returned, I asked him how it had felt to walk into the hospital alone, without someone holding his hand and supporting him.

"It was fine," he calmly and matter-of-factly replied.

Jake knew he hadn't been alone because he believed the Lord had been with him.

> The Lord himself goes before you and will be with you; he will never leave you nor forsake you. Do not be afraid; do not be discouraged. (Deuteronomy 31:8)

IN THE WAITING ROOM CALLED PRAYER

> Then Jesus told his disciples a parable to show them that they should always pray and not give up. He said: "In a certain town there was a judge who neither feared God nor cared what people thought. And there was a widow in that town who kept coming to him with the plea, 'Grant me justice against my adversary.'" (Luke 18:1–3)

LUKE RECORDED THIS parable in the first century during a time when widows in Jerusalem often had no special protection or means of financial support. In addition, if the widow didn't have a son to advocate for her, she was required to represent herself in court.

Most likely this widow didn't have a son, which is why she was seen pleading her own case in court.

Initially, the judge refused the widow's request. But because she kept coming back to court, the judge eventually gave in.

> But finally he said to himself, "Even though I don't fear God or care what people think, yet because this widow keeps bothering me, I will see that she gets justice, so that she won't eventually come and attack me!" (Luke 18:4–5)

Jake and I imagined the judge mumbling under his breath when he saw this woman come again into his courtroom. "Oh! You again!" It was with his own needs in mind that the judge finally gave in to her.

According to this biblical account, after Jesus pointed out the judge's self-centred behaviour He continued with these encouraging words: "And will not God bring about justice for his chosen ones, who cry out to him day and night?" (Luke 18:7)

Jesus's words are worth repeating. His chosen ones. His children. Day and night. At any time, day or night. When we cry out to Him, He hears us and He's there for us.

Jesus continued:

> Will he keep putting them off? I tell you, he will see that they get justice, and quickly. However, when the Son of Man comes, will he find faith on the earth? (Luke 18:7–8)

Jesus's words encouraged us to persevere in our faith in the Father. We can go to Him over and over again because He listens to our prayers. He loves us. He doesn't put us off. He doesn't dismiss us like a pesky fly who won't go away. He listens and He's there for us. All the time.

So we reached out in prayer. We also reached out for prayer. We asked friends and family to pray. We sent a prayer request to the church. We sent out emails and text messages asking for prayer and thanking those who had prayed.

We reminded ourselves of His unfailing love in our lives and reminisced about the many times He had answered our prayers.

We built truths of Scriptures into our lives and reflected on the word: "I wait for the Lord, my whole being waits, and in his word I put my hope" (Psalm 130:5).

We continued to praise Him, no matter what.

> I will extol the Lord at all times; his praise will always be on my lips. (Psalm 34:1)

We made it a habit to pray just before each appointment. We purposely arrived early enough that we would have time to pray together before exiting the car. We committed Jake and his future into the Lord's hands and also asked the Lord to prepare us to receive whatever news we might be given that particular day.

We prayed between appointments.

Jake told me that he often visited the waiting room of prayer. There, he laid bare his heart before the Father. He cried out to Him in fear and doubt, worry and sadness. He felt the love of Jesus wrap His arms around him. There, in the waiting room of prayer, he felt the greatest connection with Jesus.

We also relied on the Holy Spirit to nudge others to pray. We were often amazed by the many who told us that they prayed for Jake on a daily basis. I imagined a choir of voices, their prayers resounding in four-part harmony, all entering the presence of God at the same time on Jake's behalf. I pictured God separately hearing each individual voice and prayer. I pictured Him as He listened.

We prayed.

Then we waited for Him to answer.

> Prayer: Lord, we know that You have the whole world in Your hands. We know from Your Word that not even one little sparrow falls without You knowing about it. Lord, we know that You hold us, in particular Jake, in Your hands. We know that we can trust You to help us live out however many days You have planned for us because You've got it, Lord! Thank You for Your love. In Jesus's name we pray, amen.

IN THE WAITING ROOM CALLED PATIENCE

Be still before the Lord and wait patiently for him...
(Psalm 37:7)

EARLY IN OUR marriage, Jake and I decided that we would live. We didn't want to postpone all our goals, ambitions, and dreams until retirement, knowing full well that old age and retirement may never come. After all, when Jake was only ten years old his father had died at the age of forty-nine years from a heart attack, and my mother had died at fifty-eight from cancer.

As a result, we spent time together every day. We enjoyed weekend vacations. Once every few years, we planned a longer vacation which took us to different parts of the world and provided us with a variety of experiences.

One of our favourite vacations was a cruise through the Panama Canal. While on this fourteen-day journey, we travelled on two oceans, passed through the canal, and saw well over ten countries. While aboard the ship, we enjoyed lectures regarding the history and hardships that were faced in the canal's construction. Typically, the ship travelled at sea during the night and then docked on a new island each morning. This allowed the passengers the option to disembark on a new island every day, meet the people, see the markets, and if desired experience an onshore excursion.

One evening, we went to the purser's desk in order to arrange an onshore excursion for the following day. Others were in line ahead of us, so we were required to wait our turn.

A man stood behind us without saying a word. But his body language spoke loud and clear of his impatience. He quickly tapped his toe, rolled his eyes, and huffed while he folded his arms. He snapped his tongue off the roof of his mouth and made unintelligible comments under his breath.

His impatience annoyed me. I wanted to tell him to relax. But because I was concerned about appearing rude, I held my tongue and asked myself how I should handle this situation.

Finally, I turned to him. With a twinkle in my eye and a smile on my face, I kindly asked, "Going somewhere?"

He found my query to be rather humorous. Which it was! After all, we were in the middle of the Caribbean Sea, someone else was steering the ship, and all we had to do was sit back and relax!

Jake had always been the patient one in our relationship. He was a patient father with our daughters. He was the epitome of patience in public, in particular with those who served us. He never demanded his own way, never had a sense of entitlement, and never expected to be treated as the most important. He innately knew that conflict had the potential to arise out of impatience. He always found a better way to handle frustrating situations.

I tried to learn from Jake's quiet example. I learned that I could calm my impatience when I found a solution to a problem. Other times, I learned to be assertive and polite. In still other situations, when things were out of my control, I had no choice but to be patient and wait.

I had noticed, however, that my impatience surfaced when I sensed an injustice. At times I experienced the appearance of inadequate staff to support the growing demands of our healthcare system.

On one occasion, in my efforts to speak to someone on the phone, I got caught in a system where I was bounced from one extension to another due to people's unavailability. I verbalized my extreme frustration and impatience to Jake.

"There's no need to get upset," he calmly replied.

At that, I recognized that getting upset wasn't helping the situation. Rather, it made me feel worse.

As Jake continued in his battle with cancer, he knew that it was unhelpful to get agitated and impatient with treatments and medical appointments.

"The people helping us didn't create cancer, nor did they create the medical system," he said to me one day. "We need to be patient."

In his letter to the Romans, Paul reminds us, "Be joyful in hope, patient in tribulation, faithful in prayer" (Romans 12:12).

This became a great reminder for us—in particular, for me. I knew that my husband was suffering in this battle, but somehow I felt the need to fight on his behalf.

One day, I recognized that the fight wasn't mine. I realized that I needed to calm down, be patient, and wait for the Lord. If I did that, I would experience His hand at work in our lives, no matter what that looked like.

The Lord will fight for you; you need only to be still. (Exodus 14:14)

WAITING TO BE HEALED

> News about him spread all over Syria, and people brought to him all who were ill with various diseases, those suffering severe pain, the demon-possessed, those having seizures, and the paralyzed; and he healed them. (Matthew 4:24)

JESUS'S REPUTATION PRECEDED Him. People brought the ill to Him so He could heal them, and they did so because they believed in Him, the Healer.

Matthew, Mark, and Luke all recorded the story of a woman who had been "subject to bleeding for twelve years. She had suffered a great deal under the care of many doctors and had spent all she had, yet instead of getting better she grew worse" (Mark 5:25–26).

According to Levitical law, this poor woman was considered unclean and was therefore unable to touch or to be touched by anyone. Mark said that she had suffered this way for twelve years!

As hard as this was, she persevered and tried everything she could to get well. But unfortunately, she grew worse.

Then she saw Jesus.

When she saw Him, she told herself, "If I just touch his clothes, I will be healed" (Mark 5:28).

She was faced with a choice: touch Jesus, render Him unclean, and be healed or not touch Him and continue in her suffering.

She made a decision. She took the risk and touched the edge of His cloak.

Jesus knew someone had touched Him because "the power had gone out of him" (Mark 5:30). When Jesus called her out of the crowd, Luke tells us that she "came trembling and fell at his feet" (Luke 8:47).

Rather than chastise her for touching Him, Mark tells us that Jesus spoke to this woman and said, "Daughter, your faith has healed you. Go in peace and be freed from your suffering" (Mark 5:34).

When I reflected on this woman, I initially wondered how her faith could have been so strong... strong enough that she believed she would be healed simply by touching the hem of Jesus's cloak. In many ways, this woman's faith made me question my own, because I had asked Jesus to heal Jake and it had not happened. As a result, I believed my faith wasn't strong enough.

However, upon deeper and prayerful reflection, I realized that it wasn't this woman's faith that had brought her healing; it was her faith in the Healer that made her whole again. At that, I took the focus off me and the strength or weakness of my faith, and I placed it where it belonged—on Jesus, the Healer. I continued to earnestly ask for healing for Jake and begged the Lord to take the cancer away. I put my hope in Him at the same time that I leaned closer to Him as the Healer.

One day Jake told me that he, too, had been praying in this manner. He asked the Lord on many occasions to heal him, pleading for the cancer to be removed from his body.

We knew that Jake's healing could come in many forms. Perhaps instantaneously. Perhaps slowly. We also knew we couldn't do without the expertise and support of the many nurses and doctors who were responsible for Jake's care and treatment.

But many times we felt helpless and at the mercy of the medical system. It was exhausting! There was always one more appointment to attend, one more test, or one more medication that might help. We stuck it out. Even though we believed in the possibility that healing could come through medicine, we fully believed that ultimately Jesus was the Healer. After all, it was He who created medicine.

Jake continued to battle cancer at the same time that he struggled emotionally. One of his biggest struggles was the ongoing harassing thoughts of wondering where the cancer was in his body. As hard as he tried, some days he just couldn't find a way to make those thoughts go away.

Finally, within that emotional pain, he acquiesced to the One who knew it all and put his faith in the Healer.

"God's got it!" Jake told me. "Should I be healed and live a longer life, then God's got that. He's in control. But should I die from cancer, whenever that might be, then God's got that too! Either way, I will be healed. God's got it!"

Prayer: Lord Jesus, we praise You for being the Healer. Thank You for reminding us that our faith needs to be in You, the Healer. So we again ask for your healing hand on Jake's body while we reach out and touch the edge of your cloak. In Jesus's name we pray, amen.

IN THE WAITING ROOM CALLED SUFFERING

> And we boast in the hope of the glory of God. Not only so, but we also glory in our sufferings, because we know that suffering produces perseverance; perseverance, character; and character, hope. And hope does not put us to shame, because God's love has been poured out into our hearts through the Holy Spirit, who has been given to us. (Romans 5:2–5)

JAKE WAS VERY aware that everyone suffers and no one escapes suffering. He knew that many suffer from persecution, atrocities of war, hunger, poverty, illness, homelessness, and injury. He had the keen ability to put his suffering in perspective, knowing that many have suffered greater than he.

Having said that, he couldn't deny that he, too, suffered physically. His body had been through major surgery and radiation, which caused long-term effects on his body. Every day he battled with exhaustion.

He also suffered with his own thoughts. He worried about the cancer and where it was. This caused him much anxiety and distress, creating emotional ups and downs that affected his mental well-being.

As much as he tried to stay focused on his faith, some days he struggled spiritually. He felt tension between knowing God is love (John 4:16) and the fact that he had cancer. Jake told me that this caused him to occasionally argue with God: "If You really cared about me, Lord, why am I suffering from prostate cancer?"

In his letter to the Romans, Paul stated that we "boast in the hope of the glory of God" and also "in our sufferings" (Romans 5:2–3). It was understandable that we should boast in the hope of the glory of God.

But Paul's concept about boasting in our suffering sounded absurd. Boast in our suffering? How could we boast in our suffering and why would we want to?

A closer reflection of this verse offered clarity. Paul didn't say that we should boast because of our suffering, but that we can still boast, even while we are in our suffering, of what we have in the glory of God.

Indeed, we can still be glad in our suffering. Why? Because while in that suffering we were drawn closer to the Lord, our hope and our Healer.

The woman who suffered for twelve years went to Jesus when she saw Him. Likewise, when we're in our suffering we go to Him and touch the edge of His cloak.

Paul continues in Romans to write that suffering produces perseverance. Therefore, perseverance is a product of suffering.

We boasted in the hope of the glory of God.

Jake persevered.

While we waited.

IN THE WAITING ROOM CALLED PERSEVERANCE

CANADA'S SOUTHERNMOST TIP is located in Point Pelee National Park. Just half an hour from our home, its forest of oak, maple, and black walnut trees provides shelter to a wide variety of birds, including the blue jay, owls, woodpeckers, and the American bald eagle. Point Pelee's well-groomed beaches, marsh boardwalk, and visitor centre all offer fun and education about the wildlife and marsh creatures who make this park their home.

A few years prior to Jake's diagnosis, this beautiful park hosted a racewalk fundraiser for the local diabetes association. This was the first racewalk in which Jake and I both participated.

The temperature was perfect this beautiful spring morning, and the setting was magnificent. We waited at the starting line along with several hundred others. When the horn blared, we stepped out together.

But within about ten seconds, Jake's competitive spirit kicked into gear. He found it difficult to hold himself back to my slower pace and shorter stride.

I recognized his frustration.

"Go!" I said.

It was all he needed to hear. Like a jet taking off on a runway, his strength and stride burst out, propelling him forward. I was unable to keep up.

Thirty-eight minutes later, Jake crossed the finish line. He received a plaque for being the first in his age category to complete the five-kilometre walk. Everyone was proud of him. I crossed the finish line approximately seventeen minutes later.

Jake was hooked. Several months later, he signed up for another racewalk. Once again, he was the first in his age category to cross the finish line. However, the judges changed his category from a walk to a run, because he hadn't maintained the requirement for walkers to keep at least one foot on the ground.

The Waiting Room

He didn't win that race. But he was pleased that he had done so well. I was also very proud of him for this accomplishment.

Three years following his prostatectomy, Jake again registered for a race-walk at Point Pelee National Park. It consisted of a five-kilometre loop which headed down the main road, turned into the forest, then circled back to the finish line. Our eldest daughter had registered for the fifteen-kilometre race, which required her to run the same loop three times. This meant there was a likelihood that she would pass her father on at least two occasions. This was, of course, dependent on their individual speeds.

I waited near the finish line with my son-in-law and grandson. Each time she passed me, she gave the thumbs-up and told me the kilometre marker where she had last seen her father.

When she passed me the second time, I knew that Jake was getting close to finishing the race.

I waited and watched in anticipation for Jake to come around the bend. When he did, he had his sights focused on the finish line. He continued to put one foot in front of the other. I saw the determination on his face. He crossed the finish line with abundant joy!

But from my perspective, he was a sad sight. He walked with a gait which caused him to lean over to his right side. He struggled with every step as he forcefully swung his right arm in an effort to push himself forward. I was very concerned about him.

When the race officials suggested that the paramedics attend to him, he insisted that he didn't need help.

He was overjoyed that he had finished, even if it meant that his final time was nearly double the time of the first race-walk he had completed three years previous. I was very proud of him for his accomplishment. Despite all he had been through, he had persevered and succeeded.

But my heart broke. It was so apparent that his mind had been willing, but his body had grown weak. Even in that weakened body, he was determined to finish the race—and he did so because he kept his eyes on the finish line.

Likewise, in the race against cancer, Jake has continued to persevere. He has persevered through surgery, radiation, and hormone therapy. He has been able to persevere because he's kept his eyes on the finish line, Jesus, who gives him the physical and emotional strength he needs.

In the book of Hebrews, we are encouraged us to fix our eyes on Jesus so we won't become tired and discouraged.

> Therefore, since we are surrounded by such a great cloud of witnesses, let us throw off everything that hinders and the sin that so easily entangles. And let us run with perseverance the race marked out for us, fixing our eyes on Jesus, the pioneer and perfecter of faith. For the joy set before him he endured the cross, scorning its shame, and sat down at the right hand of the throne of God. Consider him who endured such opposition from sinners, so that you will not grow weary and lose heart. (Hebrews 12:1–3)

Jesus endured the cross and scorned its shame, then sat at the right hand of the throne of God because of the joy that was set before Him. What was that joy? It was us! He died for us and He's at the finish line, waiting. Waiting for Jake. He's standing there waiting for all of us to finish this race called life.

In the meantime, we wait for Him.

He is standing there.

Waiting for us.

IN THE WAITING ROOM CALLED CHARACTER

WE RECENTLY MADE an online purchase of a new shelf unit. It arrived in a very large box which was neatly packed and organized. It included everything needed to assemble the shelf: step-by-step instructions, diagrams, shelves, metal frames, nuts, and bolts. Each part was meticulously labelled with a number that correlated to the diagrams.

When we opened the box, several small pieces of paper fell out. They appeared to have been haphazardly thrown into the box. They read something to the effect of "Inspected by #1234." Apparently the product had been inspected for the quality of its parts as well as to ensure that all the parts had been included. In essence, the company had given its stamp of approval before the product was shipped to the purchaser. This was, of course, done to ensure that the product would retain its character and quality once assembled.

When we had finished assembling our new shelf unit, we stood it on end. But even though the shelf appeared to have been assembled properly, it needed to be tested for its purpose and quality of its character before it could be used to hold our treasures.

The moment of truth came when we placed our items on the shelves and it didn't crumble under the weight. It stood strong and was approved for its purpose.

In his letter to the Romans, Paul states that perseverance produces character.

> ...but we also glory in our sufferings, because we know that suffering produces perseverance; perseverance, character; and character, hope. (Romans 5:3–4)

Careful inspection of the word character takes us to its Greek root, dokimos, which simply means "approved, tried."[8]

In the first century, pottery was inspected for cracks after it was put through the fire. If the pottery met the required standard for its use, it was stamped dokimos. In other words, approved.

Based on the Greek word for character, we could rewrite Romans 5:3 to read: "suffering produces perseverance and perseverance, approval." But James broadens our understanding of perseverance by saying that the testing of our faith develops perseverance:

> Consider it pure joy, my brothers and sisters, whenever you face trials of many kinds, because you know that the testing of your faith produces perseverance. Let perseverance finish its work so that you may be mature and complete, not lacking anything. (James 1:2–4)

Therefore, the testing of our faith develops because of perseverance. This is the same testing that often comes following the trials and suffering. It's the testing that gives us the stamp of approval. In other words, when we consider the words character and approval to be interchangeable, we are saying that the testing of our faith gives us character.

Like the clay pots that were approved for their purpose after going through the fire, our approval or character is granted once we have persevered through the testing of our faith.

So how do we as people get that stamp of approval? After all, we cannot approve of ourselves.

The simple answer is that our approval comes from Him.

> Rather, join with me in suffering for the gospel, by the power of God. He has saved us and called us to a holy life—not because of anything we have done but because of his own purpose and grace. (2 Timothy 1:8–9)

---

[8] Ibid., 2144.

> This righteousness is given through faith in Jesus Christ to
> all who believe. (Romans 3:22)

We wondered to ourselves, Why do we need to be approved anyway? Quite frankly, we could have done without the suffering of Jake's cancer. What purpose is there in developing quality of character or approval in our lives?

Just as our shelf unit was approved for its character and quality, and just as the clay pots were approved for their purpose to hold water, as believers we, too, have been approved for a purpose.

In Paul's letters to the Ephesians and Timothy, he makes it clear that when we persevere through a trial, in the end we are able to stand up strong and be marked approved. That is, approved for His purposes.

> For we are God's handiwork, created in Christ Jesus to do
> good works, which God prepared in advance for us to do.
> (Ephesians 2:10)

> Do your best to present yourself to God as one approved,
> a worker who does not need to be ashamed and who cor-
> rectly handles the word of truth. (2 Timothy 2:15)

In his letter, James tells us that when we have stood the test, and have therefore been approved, we will receive the reward.

> Blessed is the one who perseveres under trial because,
> having stood the test, that person will receive the crown
> of life that the Lord has promised to those who love him.
> (James 1:12)

Jake received a beautiful plaque which recognized him as being the winner in his age category in the first race-walk he completed. During that walk, he kept his sights on the finish line.

Following surgery and radiation, in another race-walk, his physical suffering challenged him and made him wonder whether he would finish. But he persevered, kept his eyes on the finish line, and completed the course.

When Jake struggled through emotional and physical suffering, it tested his faith in a loving God. Yet despite those times he kept his sights on the finish line. There will be a day when Jake will be reunited with his Jesus. When he is, Jesus will present him with "the crown of life that the Lord has promised to those who love him" (James 1:12).

> I have fought the good fight, I have finished the race, I have kept the faith. Now there is in store for me the crown of righteousness, which the Lord, the righteous Judge, will award to me on that day—and not only to me, but also to all who have longed for his appearing. (2 Timothy 4:7–8)

Dokimos. Character: Approved.
Until then, we wait.

IN THE WAITING ROOM CALLED A LIVING HOPE

> But the eyes of the Lord are on those who fear him, on those whose hope is in his unfailing love... (Psalm 33:18)

WE WERE UNAWARE as to the strength and endurance we would need to run this race against cancer. Many times we didn't know whether we had the needed stamina to "run with perseverance the race marked out for us" (Hebrews 12:1).

Approximately two years had passed since Jake's diagnosis. Within that period of time, he attended thirty-three rounds of radiation, had a prostatectomy, had difficulty with chest pain, and struggled with elevated glucose levels.

We also sat in many, many waiting rooms. And between these appointments, we sat in the spiritual waiting rooms in our minds, where defeat and exhaustion joined us. There, we watched, wondered, and worried.

We sat with Jesus in God's waiting room, too, where He answered our prayers with "Wait." In His waiting room, we waited on His intervention. We prayed, trusted, persevered, and hoped.

As time progressed, we realized that we needed to intentionally go to His waiting rooms, and that we needed to linger there.

We then learned anew that we needed to lean into and hold onto hope. We anticipated a hope for a cure, but ultimately it was hope in our Lord Jesus Christ that renewed our strength and provided the endurance we needed.

It goes without saying that it wasn't always easy to be hopeful. In fact, many times it felt like hope eluded us, especially when Jake's level of activity diminished. At those times, he seemed downcast in spirit. It was very difficult to see him sleep in the afternoon rather than go out. When hope felt lost, discouragement and despair goaded us on to neglect to look to the One who is hope.

The Waiting Room

One day, we were reminded of a verse in Hebrews where the author talks about hope. Interestingly enough, the word hope is used to explain faith: "Now faith is confidence in what we hope for and assurance about what we do not see" (Hebrews 11:1).

I again delved into my Greek dictionary and discovered that hope comes from the Greek word elpis, which means "to trust, and to have a confident expectation of good."[9]

This appeared to be an easy definition for hope: a confident expectation of good.

We noticed a common thread between faith, wait, and hope.

Faith referred to certain expectation. Wait was a confident expectancy. Hope is a confident expectation of good.

At times in our lives, we placed our confidence in the wrong things. Like when we blindly trusted our car's GPS, which led us back to the U.S. border just minutes after we had crossed back into Canada.

On other occasions, we put our confidence in ourselves and our own abilities, only to later discover that we had made the wrong decision.

When our girls were younger, we occasionally left them home alone for short periods of time. We told them they were expected to be good while we were gone and that we were confident they knew right from wrong. In fact, we hoped that they were mature and wise enough to do the right things while we were away.

Upon returning home, the girls were always quite happy and there never seemed to be anything amiss in our house.

However, many years later, they shared with us that while they were home alone one time they had climbed out of a bedroom window to tan on the front porch roof. Naturally, we were horrified by the thought of what could have happened to them if they'd lost their grip and slid off!

As we grew to understand the deeper meaning of hope, we knew that our confident expectation of good could only be placed in the Saviour. We learned that we had to trust only in Him to bring good into our lives. As a result, He became our hope, the outcome of the faith we had in Christ Jesus. In fact, our hope in Him was considered alive!

---

[9] Ibid., 2159.

In the Waiting Room Called a Living Hope

> Praise be to the God and Father of our Lord Jesus Christ! In his great mercy he has given us new birth into a living hope through the resurrection of Jesus Christ from the dead... (1 Peter 1:3)

A living hope! Hope that is alive!

Our confident expectation of good was in the One who loved and died for us. He alone secured for us this living hope with His death and resurrection and promise to us of eternal life.

That hope, that confident expectation of good, came alive and grew stronger as an active participant in Jake's battle against prostate cancer. Because of that hope, we had the ability to rejoice amidst the suffering.

Jesus alone is this living hope!

"I have hope that I will be healed," Jake said to me one day, "either here on this earth or ultimately when God calls me home to live with him eternally. At that time, I'll get a new body. One that won't get sick and die!"

It was hope that sustained us through Jake's battle with cancer.

We made every effort to keep our eyes focused on Him, because that was where our hope lay.

> Yes, my soul, find rest in God; my hope comes from him. Truly he is my rock and my salvation; he is my fortress, I will not be shaken. (Psalm 62:5–6)

> But as for me, I watch in hope for the Lord, I wait for God my Savior; my God will hear me. (Micah 7:7)

We hoped while we waited.

We waited with confident expectation.

> Prayer: Dear Lord, today our prayer is from Your words in the book of Romans. We ask that You help us to "boast in the hope of the glory of God. Not only so, but we also glory in our sufferings, because we know that suffering produces perseverance; perseverance, character; and character,

hope. And hope does not put us to shame, because God's love has been poured out into our hearts through the Holy Spirit, who has been given to us" (Romans 5:2–5), Thank You, Lord, for that love. In Jesus's name we pray, amen.

THE PSMA PET SCAN

No one who hopes in you will ever be put to shame...
(Psalm 25:3)

THE DOCTOR EXPLAINED that an elevated PSA was an indication that the cancer was hiding somewhere. Since Jake's PSA was going up, especially following both a prostatectomy and radiation, a PET scan, specifically designed to identify and locate the cancer, would help determine the next course of action.

He explained that a PSMA PET scan (a prostate specific membrane antigen position emission tomography scan) targets a protein which is emitted by prostate cancer.

A consult was arranged with a doctor in London by way of a video call. He obtained a thorough history from Jake and reviewed all the reports from the urologist. Arrangements were made for Jake to attend the hospital in London for this scan.

When we arrived, we were directed to the appropriate department after completing a thorough COVID-19 screening. Once there, Jake registered and was subsequently asked to have a seat in the waiting room.

Although we had never been in this waiting room, it had a sense of familiarity. Its black vinyl seats mounted on metal frames were lined up in rows facing each other. A small table sat in the corner of the room.

Other than a few empty seats, the waiting room was full. No one looked up and no one acknowledged our presence. There wasn't even a brief nod of the head. In fact, everyone in this particular waiting room seemed occupied. Some played games on their electronic devices, a few read books or magazines, and others completed paperwork assigned to them by medical staff. A few chatted softly with those who had come to support them.

The Waiting Room

As had become customary for us, once we sat in the waiting room Jake occupied himself on his phone and I took in my surroundings. I noticed that some stared blankly into what I called the dead space of no man's land. *Possibly preoccupied by their thoughts. Or trying to avoid their thoughts altogether.*

I saw a general sadness on many of their faces.

That particular day, I also noticed several people who appeared to be seriously ill. Some were extremely thin and frail. Others were completely bald or wore head coverings.

Even though I didn't have cancer, I suddenly felt a connection with this room full of strangers simply because of this cruel and unfortunate commonality.

Cancer: what a horrible word. The very sound of it was sickening.

A few minutes after Jake and I settled in, a technician entered the waiting room and explained to Jake that the hospital needed to reschedule his appointment for another day. Apparently they had run out of the contrast dye needed for the test.

Jake's deep sigh expressed frustration, disappointment, and even exhaustion. After all, he had needed to do some mental preparation to get to this appointment. The test might finally offer an explanation as to where the cancer had landed in his body.

Once Jake explained that we'd travelled more than two hours to get to the hospital, the technician offered Jake the option of waiting.

"But you need to know it may be a long wait," he said.

We decided to wait.

On our way home later that same day, Jake shared with me that the test had been rather easy. Once the dye had been injected into his vein, all he'd had to do was lie on the table while the machine scanned his body.

Several days later, the doctor telephoned to tell Jake that the scan had been clear. However, he qualified this by explaining that the PSMA scan is unable to detect small metastasis in the lymph nodes. Due to Jake's elevated PSA, the doctor believed that's where the cancer was hiding.

Once the doctor ended the phone call, I turned to Jake. "Maybe you've been healed!"

Now there was a possibility!

We returned to the waiting room of living hope.
There we waited.

> Prayer: Lord Jesus, we praise You for being the same today as You were yesterday and will be forever. Because You are our never-changing God, we know that we can always put our hope for Jake's complete healing in You. Amen.

SOMETIMES GOD MAKES HIS PEOPLE WAIT

WHENEVER I NEEDED to talk to the Lord, He was there for me. I never had to wait. He was always available. He always listened to my prayers and ministered to me with love and gentleness. Each and every time I asked Him to heal Jake, He answered my plea with a simple and loving "Wait."

But I wondered how long I would have to wait.

I was reminded of the Israelites and how they had waited in bondage in Egypt for more than four hundred years before Pharoah had let Moses and his people go. Then, after they'd crossed the Red Sea, they had wandered the desert for another forty years before entering the Promised Land.

While in the desert, the Lord told Moses to go up to see Him on Mount Sinai.

> Then Moses set out with Joshua his aide, and Moses went up on the mountain of God. He said to the elders, "Wait here for us until we come back to you. Aaron and Hur are with you, and anyone involved in a dispute can go to them."
>
> When Moses went up on the mountain, the cloud covered it, and the glory of the Lord settled on Mount Sinai. For six days the cloud covered the mountain, and on the seventh day the Lord called to Moses from within the cloud. (Exodus 24:15–16)

Moses waited for the Lord to speak to him. In fact, Moses waited in a cloud—for six days!

The Scriptures are silent as to whether Moses grew impatient during that first period of six days, or if he wondered whether he had heard God's directions correctly. We also don't know whether Moses even doubted if God would eventually reveal Himself.

I felt certain that if I had been told to go wait on a mountain, in a cloud, for six days, doubt and impatience would have joined me there, and I would have eventually left that mountain weighed down by discouragement.

But we know that Moses waited for the Lord because the Bible tells us that he stayed on the mountain for forty days and forty nights before returning to the people. During that time, the Lord ministered to him and gave him instructions for the people.

I can only imagine the encounter Moses must have had with God!

Unfortunately, while Moses was on the mountain, impatience festered in the Israelites. It took only forty days for them to grow tired of waiting for Moses's return. As a result, they forgot what the Lord had done for them and built an "idol cast in the shape of a calf" (Exodus 32:4).

When the Lord saw what the people were doing, He told Moses that his people had become corrupt: "They have been quick to turn away from what I commanded them..." (Exodus 32:8)

It's amazing that the people were so quick to give up on Moses, and on the God who had even given them visual proof that He was on the mountain with Moses.

> To the Israelites the glory of the Lord looked like a consuming fire on top of the mountain. (Exodus 24:17)

What was the Lord's purpose in making the Israelite people wait for Moses to return? I wondered. I didn't think God was about making people wait just for the sake of waiting. In fact, when God met with Moses, He had the best interests of the Israelite people at heart. After all, He had been giving Moses the ten commandments and details for building the Ark of the Covenant, among other things.

But despite seeing His presence on the mountain, and despite all the Lord had done for them by protecting them from plagues, freeing them from Egypt, and parting the waters so they could walk on dry land, the Israelites had forgotten about His faithfulness to them.

As it related to Jake's health, the Lord had clearly told me to wait for Him to answer my prayer. While in that waiting, I had the choice to either become stronger in my faith as I drew closer to Him or, like the Israelites, forget all that He had done for me, become disgruntled, and perhaps even walk away from my faith in Him.

It therefore became important for me to remember those things He had already done for us so I couldn't lose sight of Him. Many times in my life He gave me visual evidence of His faithfulness and protection over me and our family. I was reminded of a time when we'd travelled to the state of Delaware to visit Jake's brother and his wife. On our way home, we stopped for lunch at a restaurant in Ohio along the I-80. Although the food was good, the service was extremely slow. Jake was anxious to get home again and the girls looked forward to going to their YAC (Youth After Church) event and seeing their friends.

Unfortunately, we were detained due to the poor service.

Shortly after getting back onto the highway, traffic came to a complete stop, heightening the girls' disappointment.

"Now what?" one of them asked.

Then the evidence was presented to us. While we waited for traffic to move again, a flatbed truck carrying a severely crashed car drove down the highway going in the opposite direction. We had been stopped for a reason.

Jake took this as an opportunity to encourage the girls. "Remember how frustrated we were because we had to wait at the restaurant? Just imagine if we had left the restaurant when we wanted to. It could've been us in that accident!"

Everyone calmed down at the realization that we had possibly been spared. God had protected us. We saw that He sees the bigger picture and knows what's best for us.

As we waited on Him in Jake's ongoing battle with cancer, we tried to remember those times when He didn't make us wait for waiting's sake. His plan was to provide for and protect us while we waited.

We continued to wait on Him. While we remembered.

Prayer: Lord, despite seeing Jake suffer and having to persevere through this difficult battle with cancer, we praise You for Your goodness to us. Forgive us for those times when we've complained rather than remember what You've done for us. You asked us to wait and we're trying to be patient in that waiting. But there are days when despair weighs us down. We therefore ask for Your protection over us, to keep us from falling into the temptation of lingering with discouragement rather than the hope You offer us. Thank You for loving us! Lord, we love You, even while we wait. In Jesus's name we pray, amen.

CN TOWER

THE CN TOWER is one of the greatest manmade wonders of the world. When it was constructed in 1975 in downtown Toronto, the tower was considered the world's tallest free-standing structure, standing at 553.3 metres high.[10]

When our girls were teens, we took the opportunity to visit the CN Tower. After we paid our entrance fee, we took the elevator 342 metres up to one of the observation decks. Although I was aware that some parts of the deck would have a glass floor, it still caused fear to well up in me when I realized I was able to look straight down to the ground below.

Needless to say, I avoided those sections and rather chose to walk around the outside wall of the deck, holding onto the handrail and taking in the breathtaking views.

When we looked north, we took in the city's skyscrapers. When we looked south, we saw the Toronto Islands in Lake Ontario. Other views showed us the Toronto Blue Jays' SkyDome and Highway 401, which wound its way around the city, its clover leaf turnoff lanes and bridges allowing traffic to move in all directions. From our height, the cars below appeared as little ants on the ground.

I stood beside our oldest daughter and pointed out a car on the highway. Several kilometres in front of it, we could see traffic at a complete stop while emergency vehicles attended to what appeared to be an accident. We realized that, from our perspective, we could see both the car and the accident. But we knew there was absolutely no way for the driver of that car to see that far ahead and know that it would have to come to a full stop.

For a split second, we were filled with awe as we considered what it might be like for God, who looks down upon the earth and sees it all. Except He sees everything at once. He knows about the accident ahead of the car.

---

[10] Currently it is the tenth tallest free-standing structure.

He knows who drives the car, where it's going, how much gas it has, and whether it has time to wait for the accident to clear.

And amazingly, He is also aware and present with each and every one of those who were involved in the accident, or waiting because of it, or coming up to it.

At the same time, He could see us as we watched the scene down below. He could see what was happening in the city of Toronto. He could even hear the prayers of many who might be calling out to Him, from all over the world.

"Amazing, isn't it?" I lovingly said to her. "God knows all of the twists and turns our lives will take. And He cares about each one of them."

We stood for a moment in silence while we considered our amazing God, who looks down and sees us.

> From heaven the Lord looks down and sees all mankind;
> from his dwelling place he watches all who live on earth.
> (Psalm 33:13–14)

We also knew that God has involved Himself in our lives. He loves us, hears our prayers, and lives in us.

> But God demonstrates his own love for us in this: While we were still sinners, Christ died for us. (Romans 5:8)

> For the eyes of the Lord are on the righteous and his ears are attentive to their prayer… (1 Peter 3:12)

> And we have seen and testify that the Father has sent his Son to be the Savior of the world. If anyone acknowledges that Jesus is the Son of God, God lives in them and they in God. (1 John 4:14–15)

When Jake was diagnosed with cancer, we were comforted in knowing that God sees Jake and knows what's coming next in his life.

While we waited.

Prayer: Dear Jesus, we thank and praise You for being that all-seeing and all-knowing God. Thank You for seeing us, for being involved in our lives, and for being attentive to our prayers. We again ask you to heal Jake's body. As we continue through this battle, we ask for continued protection from the enemy over our thoughts of fear. Help us to trust in You. In Jesus's name we pray, amen.

NEXT STEPS

> Truly my soul finds rest in God; my salvation comes from him. (Psalm 62:1)

THE UROLOGIST TELEPHONED Jake regarding his most recent bloodwork results.

"Your PSA has continued to climb," Dr. King stated before further explaining that this was an indication that we needed to start one of two additional hormone therapy medications.

The first was an oral medication called apalutimide. He had referred Jake to see a medical oncologist who would monitor the administration of this drug. This was of course contingent on whether Jake met the province's health insurance plan's criteria to receive it.

The second treatment was an injection to be administered once every three months, designed to shut down the production of testosterone. Dr. King explained that prostate cancer is fuelled by testosterone, so depriving the body of this hormone causes the cancer to shrink, or at least to spread less rapidly. He then reviewed the many side effects of the hormone therapy, which would include hot flashes, mood swings, weight gain, loss of libido, fatigue, and osteoporosis.

Jake attended the doctor's office the following week for his first injection.

As normal, he registered at the front desk of the doctor's office while I stood nearby. Then I followed my husband to the waiting room across the hall. He chose two empty seats on the far side of the room.

This was a waiting room we had sat in on several occasions before. But on this particular day I was taken aback by the room's layout. In an attempt to minimize the spread of COVID, the seats had been separated by approximately four feet and a tall plexiglass wall stood between each one.

The Waiting Room

I had mentally prepared myself for this next step in Jake's treatment, but I was suddenly overwhelmed by the realization that we were dealing with COVID and cancer at the same time.

"Cancer and COVID, Lord?" I asked.

Anxiety rose up in me as fear reared its ugly head and stared me in the face. The last thing I wanted for my husband was cancer; the thought of him possibly contracting COVID on top of that felt like too much!

I sat down next to Jake. My face flushed and my heart raced as I looked over at him. But he seemed unaffected by the changes in the room and totally oblivious to the angst I felt. I took some deep breaths while trying to distract myself by looking around. Even though everyone wore a mask, including myself, I smiled at a man sitting across from Jake. From the glint in his eyes and the rising of his cheekbones, I knew he smiled back at me.

In the quiet of my spirit, I heard a passage of Scripture: "Where can I go from your Spirit? Where can I flee from your presence?" (Psalm 139:7)

I knew there was nowhere to go and I didn't want to get away from God. In fact, I knew He was sitting right there beside me. Beside us! He was with us every step of the way. That alone made me feel more relaxed.

"Jacob Martens."

We knew the drill. Register. Wait. Hear your name. Rise. Follow the voice.

Jake got his first shot of hormone deprivation therapy that day. Dr. King explained to us that he would give us a prescription for the medication. In turn, once every three months we would pick up the medication and attend his office the following week, at which time Jake would receive the injection.

We went home and waited for the hormone therapy to start working.

> The Lord is near to all who call on him, to all who call on him in truth. (Psalm 145:18)

NEW LEARNING

DR. KING ALWAYS greeted us in a polite and friendly manner. In addition, he treated Jake respectfully and with dignity.

But as respectful as Dr. King had always been, there were still times when all sense of dignity was lost. After all, when it's time for a shot in the buttocks, you loosen your pants, drop your drawers, and lean over. Just like that.

When the doctor had been explaining how often Jake would receive the hormone therapy injections, he said something like this: "I'll then give you the shot in your buttocks, and off you'll go."

When we got back to the car following that appointment, Jake turned to me: "Buttocks! I just realized that's where the word butt comes from!"

WAITING IN LINE

Lord, be gracious to us; we long for you. Be our strength every morning, our salvation in time of distress. (Isaiah 33:2)

SEVERAL DAYS LATER, we again headed into the city for Jake's appointment with the medical oncologist regarding whether Jake would be prescribed apalutimide.

Although our nerves always felt a little rattled whenever we attended an appointment at the cancer centre, the presence of the friendly staff and volunteers calmed our anxiety. From the time we arrived until we left the building, we always felt supported, cared for, and cared about.

That caring and friendly attitude started the moment we arrived at the parking lot where we were greeted by the attendant. We had grown fond of her; she was an absolute delight! She knew the parking lot well and always pointed out exactly how many spots were available in each section of the lot: "Seventeen over there and twelve right here. Take your pick!"

But on this particular day, that attendant wasn't working. Her replacement was doing his best to direct traffic and move the cars in and out in an expedient manner. When we arrived, several cars were lined up on the road waiting for their turn to enter. We took our place in line and waited. It was apparently a busy day.

Suddenly, a car came from the opposite direction and abruptly turned left in front of the first car in line. The driver in that vehicle blared his horn, slammed on the brakes, exited his pickup truck, and yelled what-fors. An explosive argument ensued between the parties with a rapid exchange of expletives and flailing arms. We watched in fear, worried things would escalate and get physical.

We felt relieved when a security guard arrived and both drivers calmed down.

Then we parked and walked hand in hand into the cancer centre.

Tension walked with us.

Confusion and unfamiliarity greeted us as soon as we entered the centre's double doors. Where were the usual friendly volunteers?

The once open and airy waiting room had been converted into a COVID screening area. We were immediately handed masks and shields with firm instructions to put them on.

The first screener we approached asked Jake for his health card and confirmed his birthdate.

Well, at least that hasn't changed, I thought.

Jake put his health card away.

He was directed to another clerk, who asked him why he was in the building. He explained that he had an appointment with Dr. Jones. When she asked to see his health card, he again pulled it out of his pocket and handed it to her. As was Jake's character, he waited patiently for her to ask him for his birthdate. She placed a band on his wrist, confirmed with me that I wasn't ill, and gave him directions to the doctor's office on the second floor.

We found our way to Dr. Jones's office.

When Jake approached the registration desk, the clerk looked up. "Name."

"Dr. Jones."

The clerk giggled. "No, sir. I need your name."

Jake told her his name, after which she asked him for his birthdate.

Honestly! It hasn't changed since we walked in the door...

That's when I realized that these private parties of mine over his birthdate were really a way for me to cope with all the ongoing medical appointments. But on this day, Jake being asked for his birthdate at least brought me a sense of normalcy.

The clerk handed him a clipboard with a questionnaire and asked him to return it once he had completed the form.

When he finished, he took the clipboard back to the receptionist. She giggled again.

"Sir. I also need the form you completed."

Once he returned the form, she asked him to have a seat in the waiting room.

Within a few minutes, a nurse came out and called Jake's name. When he rose, she asked him for his birthdate. I giggled.

She led us to an exam room where we waited for the doctor.

The doctor was very calm and kind. After asking a few screening questions, he said that he needed to do a series of blood tests. Before he could prescribe the oral therapy, he needed to first substantiate a consistent increase in Jake's PSA over a three-week period.

He further explained that since Jake had already started on the hormone therapy, there was a possibility this could already have lowered his PSA. That, of course, would be seen as a good thing; it would mean that the hormone therapy was doing its job and this particular medication wouldn't be needed.

At the end of the appointment, Jake was directed to the hospital lab for bloodwork.

When we arrived at the lab, we were once again faced with a COVID protocol. The hallway outside the lab had been converted into a waiting room. Chairs lined only one side of the hallway, each of them six feet apart.

A few people waited for their names to be called. There was no interaction. Everyone sat in silence.

Eventually, Jake's name was called. I was left alone in the hallway.

But I wasn't alone. I knew the Lord was with me every step of the way. I believe Jesus sat right there beside me. He sat with me in my agitation and bewilderment. He even sat with me in my private parties.

For the next few weeks, Jake attended weekly for bloodwork. The good news was that his PSA didn't rise during this time, most likely because the hormone therapy had started to do its job. As a result, it wasn't necessary for Jake to be placed on this oral therapy.

At that point, the treatment plan for him was to continue on the hormone therapy.

While we watched and waited.

The Waiting Room

Prayer: Thank You, Lord, for being our strength this morning. Thank You for always being with us. We continue to wait on You. In Jesus's name we pray, amen.

PRAYING AND WAITING

> I am worn out calling for help; my throat is parched. My eyes fail, looking for my God. (Psalm 69:3)

I AWAKENED EARLY. The house was quiet.

My thoughts immediately went to a sad place. Sadness about Jake. When would this end? When would we finally be able to say that he was healed?

We had been praying for a miracle.

Praying.

Waiting.

Praying and waiting.

I heard a small voice: "You're angry about many things, aren't you?"

I knew it wasn't a question.

"Lord!" I knew He was there, speaking to me through His Spirit.

I didn't feel chastised. Rather, I knew the Lord was there with me, in my pain and sadness.

In an effort to be strong for my husband, I had stuffed down my emotions in a dark cavernous place deep inside my heart. I knew my husband well enough to know he would blame himself if he knew I felt sad, even though he had no control over the cancer or how I handled my emotions.

I prayed to the Lord as I lay quietly beside Jake. It was a prayer of deep anguish. My eyes cried no tears, but my heart wept.

"Yes, Lord," I answered Him. "I am very angry!"

My anger intensified as I revealed to Him the depth of my pain.

"I'm angry that Jake has cancer, and that he has to go through so much. I'm angry that we continue to have to wait for appointments and tests and answers. I'm angry because it feels like no one understands what I'm feeling or what we're going through. Lord, I feel so alone."

It felt good to share this with Him. I knew that He understood.

"I'm angry because I need to hug my children and grandchildren, but I can't because of COVID. I'm angry because what Jake needs right now is a hug from his children and grandchildren. I'm angry because Jake has done nothing to deserve this! Prostate cancer, Lord?"

I heard Jesus respond: "And I did nothing to deserve being crucified. But I did it for you."

I knew Him well enough to know that He was just lovingly reminding me that He had died for my sin, and for my pain.

I reached out and felt His hand in mine. I felt His arms of love wrap around me.

I fell asleep.

I awoke a short while later as a bright light filled our bedroom.

"Lord?"

I felt His presence sitting at the foot of our bed. "Hang on tight. You're in for a rough ride. But I'll be there with you every step of the way."

> "The Lord is my light and my salvation—whom shall I fear? The Lord is the stronghold of my life—of whom shall I be afraid...
>
> Wait for the Lord; ne strong and take heart and wait for the Lord. (Psalm 27:1, 14)

Wait for the Lord.
Be strong and take heart.
Wait with confident expectation.
Wait for the Lord.

Prayer: Lord Jesus, thanks for listening. Thanks for loving me. Amen.

IN THE AIRPORT WAITING ROOM

We wait in hope for the Lord; he is our help and our shield.
(Psalm 33:20)

EVENTUALLY, THE WORST of COVID dissipated and services and stores reopened. We took this as a window of opportunity to fly to Alberta to see our daughter and her family. Jake found an affordable direct flight from Hamilton to Calgary, which meant we were required to drive three hours from our home to Hamilton. The price was right, so we decided to made it work.

We arrived at the airport, checked in, went through security, and then waited for our flight to be called while we sat in the appropriate waiting area.

We had always enjoyed watching people at the airport and this day was no different. The face mask requirement had produced new fashion statements; some were homemade, some were medical grade, and others even looked like Donald Duck! We noticed many people wearing glasses with their face masks. Then there were those who also wore a hat. Occasionally, a few people wore all three!

People took their seats and busied themselves on their devices, chatted with others, or just took in the activity all around them. A few cared for the elderly while others attended to the needs of small children. A few travelled alone.

Time passed quickly. Before we knew it, it was almost time for us to board. Many arose and stretched their legs. Others headed to the washroom.

That's when Jake turned to me and said that he needed to change his incontinence pad before boarding.

"Okay." My reply was simple and matter-of-fact. I didn't know why he was announcing to me that he needed to take care of his personal business. I expected that he would head to the washroom.

The Waiting Room

Rather than rise, he leaned in close. "I don't have any supplies left."

He looked at me with the hope that I would magically make one appear out of my purse. I usually had a couple, but he had already used those. I double-checked my purse to be certain but came up empty. We both felt a sense of panic when we realized we had miscalculated how many supplies he would need. We knew that without a pad he would wet through his clothes by the time we landed in Calgary.

Our luggage was well-stocked, but unfortunately it had already been checked in and was most likely on the plane.

I grew quiet and tried to focus on a solution. My thoughts raced as I frantically asked myself what to do.

Then it occurred to me that there was likely a supply dispenser in the ladies' washroom.

"I have an idea," I said, turning to Jake. "I'll be right back!"

I quickly headed to the ladies' room and purchased some supplies. It cost me two dollars, but that was okay.

Returning to Jake's side, I quietly explained to him what I had in my hand. He was shocked. He shook his head as his eyes grew big. His overall reaction told me that he was absolutely contrary to the idea.

I tried to convince him. "Basically, it's the same thing, except the ladies' pads aren't as heavy as the ones you usually use, and they're wrapped in pink instead of grey."

He listened intently and appeared to calm down.

"Don't worry," I reassured him. "It won't cause you to start a monthly!"

We both laughed at the mere thought of that on top of the hot flashes he was already having from the hormone therapy.

The airline attendant announced that it was time to prepare to board. People were sighing with relief as they gathered their carryon luggage and lined up.

Jake rushed to the washroom while I organized our few carry-ons.

While I waited for Jake, I looked out across the waiting room and guessed that there were approximately three hundred people by our gate. I did some simple math: three hundred people divided by two meant there would be approximately one hundred fifty men on the plane. I recalled that the Canadian Cancer Society estimated that one in eight men would develop prostate cancer in their lifetime and one in thirty would die from it.[11] This meant that seventeen men on this plane alone had already been diagnosed with prostate cancer or would one day battle the disease. This plane alone!

I looked towards the other end of the waiting room, where another group of people waited to board. I doubled the number to thirty-four. At that, a deep sadness fell over me. One man on these two plans had the potential of dying from prostate cancer.

Jake interrupted my thoughts. "Let's get in line," he urged.

While we waited in line, I reread the sign posted by the waiting room seats: "Please maintain distance with a minimum of two seats between passengers. Thank you for practicing physical distancing."

I laughed to myself. How ironic! We had practiced physical distancing in the waiting room, yet somehow it now seemed appropriate to pack all these people like sardines into a crowded plane!

Many of these men may end up battling prostate cancer, some of whom may lose the fight, I reminded myself, my heart feeling heavy. Maybe one day there will be a cure. We can't lose hope.

---

[11] "Prostate Cancer Statistics," *Canadian Cancer Society*. May 2024 (https://cancer.ca/en/cancer-information/cancer-types/prostate/statistics).

THE FALL

> If either of them falls down, one can help the other up. But pity anyone who falls and has no one to help them up.
> (Ecclesiastes 4:10)

MY DAUGHTER AND I heard a loud bang in the basement followed by a blood-curdling scream. We looked at each other quizzically.

"Dad!" she exclaimed.

We ran downstairs and found Jake lying on the floor in the mechanical room. His face was on the belt of the treadmill, his ribs having landed on the treadmill's corner edge. He was screaming and writhing in pain. The chair upon which he'd been standing lay tipped over. He had apparently gone downstairs to change the furnace filters. While he was at it, he'd decided to stand on a chair to change a filter on an air freshener.

I immediately checked to see where he was hurt. His arms and legs seemed fine, but I was unsure about his ribcage. With my assistance, Jake managed to rise and get into the car so I could transport him to the hospital.

After his initial examination, the emergency room doctor ordered some X-rays.

"Fortunately, no broken bones," the doctor later reported. "However, cracked ribs are sometimes difficult to see on an X-ray."

The doctor reassured us that even though Jake was prone to broken bones due to the hormone treatments, he didn't seem to be hurt anywhere else. He was actually very fortunate not to have been more seriously injured.

Then the doctor asked Jake this question: "Were you standing on a chair, on a chair, on a filing cabinet?"

Jake was very confused by the question and laughed. "No… and I don't understand what would have prompted you to ask me such an unusual question…"

The Waiting Room

Our oldest daughter was working in the emergency room that day. Apparently, prior to the doctor seeing Jake, she had told him about a time when she was younger and had watched her father rig up a series of items to climb on so he could reach something on the roof of the barn. From her best recollection, he had parked the tractor by the house, raised the bucket on the tractor as high as it would go, then placed a ladder in the bucket. She had watched her father as he climbed up onto the tractor, stepped into the bucket and then climbed up the ladder to retrieve the item on the roof of the barn. It was a miracle he hadn't fallen.

When he was discharged from emergency, Jake spent the next couple of weeks "taking it easy."

We were grateful that my daughter and I had been home that day and Jake hadn't been alone.

IF THE CANCER DOESN'T KILL HIM, I THINK I WILL!

> I keep my eyes always on the Lord. With him at my right hand, I will not be shaken. (Psalm 16:8)

THIS CHAPTER NEEDS to start with this disclaimer: I have always loved my husband and wanted what was best for him.

Initially, Jake adjusted quite easily to the hormone treatments. Other than the occasional hot flash, he had very few side effects. However, it did have an impact on his diabetes. His blood sugar levels took a sudden jump and it was difficult for him to bring them down to a safe level. This required him to go on insulin for the extra support he needed to deal with the disease.

Three months following his first injection of hormones, Jake received his second injection. The hot flashes then became more frequent and intense. Often they awakened him in the middle of the night. This sometimes caused him to sweat so profusely that he had to either change his T-shirt or remove it.

After a while, however, the hot flashes made Jake feel extremely uncomfortable. I often heard him say things like "Here's another one!" or "Oh no, here they come again!" My heart really went out to him.

I tried to encourage him by explaining that when women went through the change of life, they got hot flashes, too. But he responded by telling me that women didn't get them like he did. I attempted to convince him that he could gracefully deal with the hot flashes.

"After all, women don't talk about every hot flash they get," I said.

Then he made it very clear to me that he was not a woman. Of course, I was extremely grateful for that! We chuckled.

I encouraged him to sit and relax through the hot flashes. I also reminded him that the hot flashes weren't permanent and would subside after thirty seconds or so.

Jake tried to apply these suggestions. But after a short period, rather than verbalize that he was having a hot flash, he started to moan. At first, this new way of expressing himself frightened me because I thought he was having a heart attack. When I would turn toward him, concerned that something was dreadfully wrong, he'd snap at me: "It was just a hot flash!" I found his reactions disrespectful and frustrating.

"You're right. It's just a hot flash. It's not going to kill you!"

"I know. But they feel so horrible!"

"I get that. But let's remember: the medication is helping to keep you alive and lengthen your life. You might want to consider the hot flashes as a blessing in disguise! I agree they're uncomfortable, but they're a necessary evil. So please stop the theatrics!"

As much as I tried to help him deal with the hot flashes, I couldn't seem to find the right words of encouragement.

At the same time, my heart went out to him. As a woman, I'd often not known what to do with all the hormones racing through my body. They had changed on a biweekly basis, changing during pregnancy, and then changed again postpartum. I could only imagine how difficult it must have been for him to adjust to these drugs that not only shut down his male hormones but replaced them with hormones completely foreign to his body.

Approximately nine months after starting this therapy, we noticed that Jake lacked energy. He was extremely tired and slept a lot. It was an effort for him to do anything requiring physical exertion. Going for a walk most days was an effort. The doctor told us this was most likely due to the low testosterone. Testosterone is what gives a man energy.

Around this time, I also noticed a significant change in Jake's personality. In addition to his emotions running in every direction, my once gentle, quiet, and extremely patient husband became verbally aggressive, impatient, and angry.

The increase in anger started gradually. He would respond to me abruptly, sometimes with a short attitude and impatience. I attributed this low-grade anger to the exhaustion he felt from lack of testosterone. But since the therapy was also affecting his libido, I wondered whether the anger was partly due to him adjusting to that loss in his life.

But within a short period of time, his anger worsened. He would have mini-explosions over the littlest things. I tried not to ruffle his feathers, but this had a huge impact on our emotional intimacy. When he snapped at me, I spoke up for myself and let him know I didn't appreciate being spoken to in that manner.

Sometimes his demands were bizarre and came out of left field. There was no way for me to anticipate what might come next.

For example, one night I left the bathroom door ajar after rising to use it. Since he slept on the side of the bed closest to the bathroom door, the light bothered him. But rather than slipping out of bed to close the door, he demanded that I get out of bed and do it, which I did. But when I crawled back into bed, he still wasn't satisfied. He demanded I get back up and adjust the door so it was only open four inches. It was such a bizarre request, and certainly unlike him. I felt somewhat disgruntled by this, but didn't push it, given that it was the middle of the night.

Once I returned to bed, though, I laid awake for a long while wondering where my husband had done. We had been married for forty-three years, and for the first time in our relationship I felt lost. I didn't know what to do or how to handle some of these situations.

Approximately one year after his first injection, Jake was a very different man from the man I had married. I walked on eggshells while waiting for him to react to whatever it was that he felt I had said or done wrong. His verbal attacks came out of nowhere.

His impatience, too, got worse. This man who had always been extremely tolerant and calm with me, our children, and grandchildren became the epitome of impatience.

Anger intensified in him. He raised his voice at me over the littlest things. When he did, I tried my best to affirm his right to feel angry while at the same time telling him he didn't have the right to speak to me that way.

It didn't seem to matter what I said. Nothing had an impact on his behaviour.

Then it happened: a venomous explosion that caught me totally off-guard.

As we had done on many occasions, we were together in the kitchen preparing food. I had placed a cutting board on the counter beside the sink

The Waiting Room

so he could cut some vegetables. I stood on the other end of the sink, mixing ingredients in a bowl. At one point, I stepped towards him and asked him to shift over slightly so I could throw some eggshells in the garbage. He stood with his feet firmly planted and adamantly refused. When I asked him again to move two inches so I could get at the garbage, he yelled at me and in no uncertain terms told me I needed to make up my mind. After all, I had asked him to stand in that spot to cut up the carrots and he wasn't about to move.

When I pointed out that I had just asked him to shift over a few inches, he whipped the sharp knife into the sink and stormed out of the kitchen.

Horrified and shocked, overwhelmed and discouraged, I slumped into a chair.

I can't do this anymore, I thought, feeling emotionally exhausted. I didn't know which way to turn. I questioned myself, wondering what I had done wrong and whether I should've done something differently. I was deeply troubled. What had happened with my loving, kind, and patient husband?

In anguish, I quietly prayed: "Lord, what do I do?"

Immediately, peace washed over me and I heard a little voice speak. "It's the hormones."

In that instant, I realized that Jake's behaviours weren't directed to me personally.

Several days later, Jake had an appointment to see the urologist. It had been a year since his first injection. As was our custom, we attended these appointments with his prescription for the injection. It had also been our practice to prepare a list of questions and concerns to raise with the doctor. This had helped us stay on top of any medical issues that had arisen since his previous appointment.

For this appointment, I purposely hadn't told Jake what I planned on telling the doctor.

When we arrived, the foyer of the hospital was relatively quiet. There were no COVID screeners, no forms to complete, and no one demanding that we wear a mask. Even the halls seemed quiet.

After Jake registered, we entered Dr. King's waiting room. It too felt quiet. There were only a few patients, two of whom were accompanied by their wives. The plexiglass dividers were still up, preventing people from talking to each other. Everyone occupied themselves with their phones.

Jake's name was called and we rose together.

Dr. King joined us a few minutes later in the exam room. Following our usual greetings, I shared my concerns. I provided him with some details regarding Jake's mood swings, which I felt had gotten totally out of hand. I had raised three daughters and taught them to find ways to control their emotions, but I was at a loss as to how I could help my husband.

Dr. King listened intently.

After I explained that this man who had never said a mean word to me in nearly forty-three years had turned into an angry and impatient person I no longer knew, the doctor immediately recommended that Jake should take a break from the hormone therapy.

"Let's make today your last shot for a while," he suggested.

Then Dr. King encouraged us. Until this point in time, the hormone deprivation therapy had done what it was supposed to do: it had suppressed the cancer by shutting down the flow of testosterone, which was the cancer's fuel. He further explained that by going off the hormone therapy, Jake's body would have an opportunity to rest and rebuild its supply of testosterone. This would help renew his energy level and restore his emotional state.

"We'll continue to monitor you with regular bloodwork to keep an eye on your PSA," the doctor said. "We will watch and wait." He then paused, looking directly at Jake. "You need to know, though, that testosterone will rise without the androgen deprivation therapy. This will give you energy, but over time the cancer will rear its ugly head. Our best indicator will be the rising PSA. When that happens, we'll put you back on hormone therapy to zap the cancer again."

We were also concerned that Jake might experience sugar lows again by going off the therapy, since the treatments had triggered a worsening of his diabetes.

"Keep an eye on it!" Dr. King recommended.

We agreed that it was a good plan to give Jake a break from the hormones, but at the same time we felt extremely nervous. It felt like we were giving the cancer the opportunity to run wild again, and we didn't know where it might land.

Nevertheless, we trusted the doctor's experience and expertise. We left his office that day with a plan.

A plan to watch and wait.

Or was it wait and watch?

We waited.

Prayer: Lord Jesus, I am so grateful that You know everything, including what's best for Jake. Lord, today I feel so overwhelmed and confused. The hormone therapy helped put the cancer to sleep, but the side effects were so difficult to deal with. Without it, there's risk the cancer will once again surface. It feels like we're in a no-win situation. Help me, Lord, to leave this all in Your loving hands and trust You. In Jesus's name, amen.

THANKING GOD WHILE WE WAITED

> Rejoice always, pray continually, give thanks in all circumstances; for this is God's will for you in Christ Jesus. (1 Thessalonians 5:16–18)

REJOICE. PRAY. GIVE thanks. The Living Bible adds some interesting emphasis to the beginning of this verse:

> No matter what happens, always be thankful, for this is God's will for you who belong to Christ Jesus. (1 Thessalonians 5:16–18, TLB, emphasis added)

When we first read that verse, we couldn't understand why we were expected to thank God for all things. Several questions rattled in our heads. Did we really need to be thankful for Jake having prostate cancer? How were we supposed to be thankful for that? What were we supposed to be thankful for?

As hard as we tried, we just couldn't find an answer to these questions. We also couldn't understand why God would ask us to give thanks in all circumstances. Always be thankful? We weren't thankful. In fact, we were often disgruntled, and sometimes even angry. We certainly weren't thankful for cancer.

We had already learned in Romans 5:3, that we should rejoice while in our suffering, not because of it. Likewise, we learned from 1 Thessalonians that God wasn't asking us to give thanks for all things, but to give thanks in all circumstances. God wasn't asking us to thank Him for the cancer, but to thank Him despite the cancer. Even in this trial, we could find ways to thank God.

Prior to his diagnosis, we rejoiced over the healing we had experienced from trauma in my childhood. We praised God for how He had walked with us through some very difficult years. We had experienced His amazing grace and abounding love and knew that He had walked with us through the difficulty.

But did we truly believe that He would walk with us through this time as well?

Despite having experienced His close presence with us then, we asked ourselves now whether we were truly prepared to thank God in this circumstance. Were we truly willing to give Him thanks in the middle of Jake's battle with cancer? Were we willing to do so no matter what, especially if He didn't answer our prayers the way we wanted them to be answered?

We knew we needed to continue to trust in our heavenly Father for all He had already done for us. We were also fully aware that there were so many things to be thankful for and to praise God for, even in this circumstance.

We thanked Him that Jake's level of pain had been minimal. Prior to the diagnosis, and occasionally throughout, he had suffered some back pain. But mostly he struggled with tiredness, weakness, and lack of energy. In fact, for the most part he rarely complained. It was therefore safe to say that his sense of suffering wasn't necessarily physical.

We thanked Him for doctors, nurses, technicians, and hospitals. The care Jake had received was phenomenal. We thanked Him for Dr. King's knowledge and experience as it related to prostate cancer and how to treat it.

We were grateful that we lived in Canada and that the cost of Jake's medication, hospital expenses, and tests were covered. We never had to worry about making a choice between paying for drugs or buying groceries.

Every morning, we praised and thanked Him for the blessing of a new day while we determined in our hearts to praise Him no matter what, despite the circumstances we faced.

> Prayer: Lord Jesus, we thank You for all that You have done for us. Even while we wait, we praise You. We praise you! While we wait. In Jesus's name, amen.

IN THE WAITING ROOM CALLED GRACE

IN HIS SECOND letter to the Corinthians, Paul shared that he had a thorn in the flesh; it had been placed there by the enemy himself. Although Paul doesn't reveal what the thorn was, on three occasions he asked the Lord to take it away. God didn't remove the thorn.

> But [God] said to me, "My grace is sufficient for you, for my power is made perfect in weakness." Therefore I will boast all the more gladly about my weaknesses, so that Christ's power may rest on me. That is why, for Christ's sake, I delight in weaknesses, in insults, in hardships, in persecutions, in difficulties. For when I am weak, then I am strong. (2 Corinthians 12:9–10)

We asked ourselves, if grace was sufficient, then what was grace?

I once heard an acronym for grace: God's riches at Christ's expense. Christ gave all of Himself, including death on the cross, so He could present us back to the Father as if we hadn't sinned.

It cost Christ all that He had. He paid the price for us.

One day, Jake explained this verse his own way. "God is saying that grace is all we need. Grace is what He gives to us. It's there all the time, in the good and the bad. In the good things we have done and also in the bad things. In the good parts of life and in our struggles. Without grace, we would have nothing. Grace is His gift to us. It's all we need."

His grace is sufficient. It's exactly what we need. Grace is the foundation upon which Christianity exists, for without grace there would be no forgiveness of sins and no promise of eternal life. Grace is the foundation upon which our faith exists. We need to lean into grace and receive that forgiveness and promise of eternal life despite what we've done.

If grace was the only thing we had, it would be sufficient.

God's message to Paul was this: "My grace is sufficient for you, for my power is made perfect in weakness." Paul reconciled this by stating that he was content with weaknesses and hardships because that was when he was strong. He relied on the Father in his weaknesses. Despite the thorn placed there by the enemy, Paul was content because he knew Christ could use the weakness so His power could be perfected.

If Jake never had a struggle, he wouldn't have had any need to rely on God. His sufficiency would have been in himself. Rather, he relied on God and His grace.

One of those weaknesses was prostate cancer.

One day, Jake received a telephone call from a man we hadn't spoken to in many years. He shared with Jake that he had been diagnosed with prostate cancer. He'd heard that Jake also had prostate cancer and wanted to talk. We immediately invited him and his wife over for a visit.

In the past, hurtful feelings between us had left our relationship fractured. Although the passage of time had healed some of those hurts, Jake and I were concerned whether our time together might still feel awkward and strained.

While the men shared their prostate cancer experiences, however, suddenly all those other things no longer mattered. The visit ended with promises to pray for one another.

Healing happened that day. Not in the men's bodies, but in their relationships. Most importantly, God's restorative power was magnified in their physical weakness.

We may never know how God can use us in our weakness, or how Jake's faith in God, no matter what, will impact others for the positive. But we do believe that He will be glorified through it all.

In our weakness, God will be glorified.

All because of His grace.

Grace was all we needed.

Grace is all we need.

THE BLUE JAYS

WE LOOKED BACK to a particular spring when we had been blessed with warmer than usual temperatures. As the grass turned green, the birds busied themselves building nests and feeding from Jake's birdfeeders in the back yard.

During one of our Sunday lunches with our children and grandchildren, Jake shared that he had seen seven bluejays in our back yard during the previous week. Everyone knew exactly what he meant and they responded with comments like "Wow!" or "That's beautiful!"

Everyone except for our six-year-old grandson.

"Were they wearing their jerseys?" he replied rather excitedly.

We all laughed. His father then explained to him that we weren't talking about the Toronto Blue Jays baseball team, but actual birds called bluejays.

"Boy!" his father said afterward. "It's a good thing they weren't the Tigers!"

EXTRA INNINGS IN THE WAITING

THIS CHAPTER IS dedicated to Jake's cousin through marriage, Paul Krueger, who passed away from prostate cancer on February 22, 2018.

In 2014, Jake and I decided to drive from our home in southern Ontario to our daughter's home in Alberta, just northwest of Calgary.

While we drove west across the country, we were awestruck by the changing landscape and beauty of the earth. We imagined hearing the voice of God as He spoke the world into existence. We pictured God as He created light in the darkness, separated the waters, and identified the sky. We envisioned Him as He held the world in His hands and pulled the dry land up out of the water. We imagined the Creator's thumbs and fingers as they moulded and shaped the hills and mountains, the flat terrain, the oceans, the rivers, the streams, and the lakes.

With every turn around every hill, we enjoyed an abundant variety of plants, trees, and vegetation. When we saw cows in the fields, horses grazing, or deer running—at one point, a baby black bear even ran across the highway in front of us!—we were reminded that God created all the animals as well.

Prior to leaving home, we had purchased a pickup truck which had a new satellite radio system. This allowed us to listen to a specific station even after we'd travelled well outside its usual broadcast area.

Jake had always been an avid baseball fan. He taught our girls how to play baseball, coached youth baseball when they were teens, and even played in a men's baseball league. So when he discovered a Toronto Blue Jays/Detroit Tigers game on the radio, he was absolutely thrilled!

This game became a perfect alternative to music and news, and kept us entertained as we drove.

But.

The Waiting Room

We had no idea that this baseball game would last more than six and a half hours.

Amazingly, the game went into extra innings. First the tenth inning, then the eleventh. We were shocked when the game continued into the seventeenth inning... and then the eighteenth! Finally, in the nineteenth inning, the Blue Jays won, 6–5.

To this day, we are certain that our screams and cheers could be heard outside our vehicle as we drove down the highway.

A few years later, we awakened early one morning to a very clear command which we knew came the Holy Spirit: "Go visit Paul. Today."

Paul was married to Jake's first cousin, Mary. He had been diagnosed with prostate cancer in April 2014. From our occasional discussions with Mary, we knew that Paul had been part of a medical trial, but we were unaware of his prognosis.

When we arrived unannounced at Paul and Mary's house, she met us at the door and welcomed us with open arms.

"Why are you here?" she asked.

Jake replied confidently. "Because God told us to come."

Mary told us that on that very morning, she had felt quite down about Paul's lack of progress. In her sadness and bewilderment, she had prayed to God: "I can't do this alone anymore. Where are you, God? Where are these people, Lord? These people who say they are praying? Cuz, Lord, I need them now."

It was a humbling experience to know that God had used us to be Jesus-with-skin-on to Mary. We weren't the only ones; several others heard Him call and visited Paul that day.

During our visit, Paul shared with us that whenever he got his bloodwork results, and got put in wait-and-watch mode, he saw it as a good thing.

"It was like getting extra innings in a baseball game," he knowingly said.

A few weeks later, God called Paul's name and he rose and followed the voice of his Saviour.

Jake was diagnosed with prostate cancer nine months later. Like Paul, each and every time Jake got blood test results back, we too celebrated those extra innings God had given him in this waiting room called life.

Wait and watch.

JESUS IN THE WAITING ROOM

THIS CHAPTER IS dedicated to Paul's wife, Mary, who walked beside him during his battle with prostate cancer. This is her story. It is also dedicated to all those who have supported their loved one battling with cancer, because they too need to know that they aren't alone.

> Therefore, since we are surrounded by such a great cloud of witnesses, let us throw off everything that hinders and the sin that so easily entangles. And let us run with perseverance the race marked out for us, fixing our eyes on Jesus, the pioneer and perfecter of faith. (Hebrews 12:1–2)

A few years after Paul passed away, we told Mary about this book, *The Waiting Room*, to which she excitedly and confidently declared, "I saw Him!"

Almost simultaneously, Jake and I both responded. "Saw who? Who'd you see?"

"I saw Jesus. I saw Him in a waiting room!"

Mary shared with us that she had seen Him at the cancer clinic in London. She explained that the clinic was set up in an atrium, with the waiting room in the middle of the space while the doctors' offices, lab, pharmacy, and chemo lab were positioned around it. Due to the high open ceiling and the windows, the clinic had a lot of light which streamed down into the middle of the waiting room.

That particular day, the sun had been bright outside and its beams of light had shone into the waiting room.

"It was as if those rays of light were brightening up that dark spot in our lives that we called cancer," she said.

The Waiting Room

Mary went on to explain that whenever Paul went for a chemo treatment, he was first required to have bloodwork. On that day, Paul had his bloodwork done, then joined her in the wait to see the doctor.

However, once he sat down he remembered that he had forgotten to complete a form on the computer. He left her alone in the waiting room while he went to do that.

"Before he got up, Paul had been sitting to my right, and to my left there was an end table" Mary recalled. "Once he walked away, I took a minute to observe the other people in the waiting room. You could tell who the patients were, and who the support people were. I looked at people's eyes. They seemed to speak of sadness and even hopelessness."

Feeling a heaviness in her spirit, Mary had prayed: "Where are You, God?"

She continued her story. "Almost immediately, I felt something brush against my left arm, and I felt a presence beside me. When I turned to look, I saw Jesus. He was sitting right there on the end table beside me. He was swinging his bare feet and had a smile on His face. He wore a tunic made of rough material, green and brown in colour. It's strange! As I share this, it feels like I'm right back there. His presence has never left me."

Mary stopped talking and took a deep breath.

"I wasn't surprised to see Him. His mere presence affirmed in me that I wasn't alone, even though many times during Paul's battle with cancer I had felt so alone. As I took in Jesus beside me, though, I noticed another woman sitting across from me. She seemed to be looking towards the place where I saw Jesus. I looked at her and wondered whether she had seen Him, too. As I tried to figure this out, a second woman approached just to the left of where Jesus sat, and in her efforts to settle herself in she put her coffee cup down right on what I saw as being Jesus's lap. That was when I knew she hadn't seen Him!" She smiled. "I spoke to Him in my spirit and asked Him about Paul: 'So what are we looking at here? Is this going to be good news?' And the Lord told me, 'No, it's not.'"

When they were then called in to see the doctor, he did indeed tell them the news wasn't good. In addition, due to Paul's bloodwork results, the doctor wasn't able to administer the chemo treatment that day and Paul's appointment would need to be rescheduled.

Mary chose to drive home because Paul was exhausted. Due to construction on Highway 401, though, she decided to take the cut off towards Ridgetown. She thought this would be a less stressful route home.

"I still remember exactly where I was when it happened," she recalled. "I remember the houses and the trees. I remember that suddenly our entire van was surrounded by angels, and they stayed with us as we travelled along. I believed it was Jesus's way of reminding me that He was still walking with us, even though the news was bad."

The next morning, while Paul still slept, Mary decided to go to the road to retrieve the newspaper. Her typical path would have taken her through the back door, then around the side of the house towards the road out front.

"That's when it happened—again. When I opened the back door, the entire yard was full of angels!" she said. "They didn't have wings, but I definitely knew they were heavenly beings because they brought me a sense of comfort and peace. Some of them were playing golf, others were in the swimming pool area, and some were talking to each other. Still others walked along the flowerbeds. I stood there for a while and watched them. Once again, this reassured me that I wasn't walking alone."

Unfortunately, when she returned from getting the newspaper the angels were gone. Paul didn't get to see them.

"It made me wonder," she continued. "Were the angels there for me? Did Jesus reveal Himself just to me because I was needing to be ministered to in that way? Was it because I needed that comfort and reassurance?"

Mary then recalled that Paul had told her that whenever he had a chemo treatment, he always felt surrounded by what he called "a cloud of witnesses." He didn't know who they were, but he did know their presence reassured him.

"I believe this was God's way of letting him know he wasn't alone, that He was there with Paul. Just like He sent the angels to reassure me."

Mary wrote down these experiences and made note of the following verse in her journal:

> Those who know your name will trust in you, for you, Lord,
> have never forsaken those who seek you. (Psalm 9:10)

The Waiting Room

We are not alone.
We are never alone.
In the waiting room.
In God's waiting room.
In the waiting room called life.

WAITING WAS A GOOD THING

But now, Lord, what do I look for? My hope is in you.
(Psalm 39:7)

JAKE AND I have both had opportunity over the years to travel, either by way of mission trips or vacations we planned for our own rest and enjoyment. We have visited a wide variety of countries including Bermuda, Bahamas, Panama, Ecuador, Guatemala, Kenya, and South Korea. These travels have broadened our worldview as it relates to people, their cultures, and their needs.

Naturally, of course, we had many opportunities to travel to Alberta to visit our daughter, her husband, and their children.

One summer, our daughter and son-in-law invited us to join them on a camping trip at Goldstream Provincial Park on Vancouver Island. They promised to provide us with a tent and food, as long as we got ourselves to Comox, British Columbia. Jake arranged for a direct flight from nearby Windsor to Calgary, with a connecting flight to Comox.

The plane left Windsor on time and headed west for its four-hour journey. We settled into our seats and kept ourselves busy by napping, reading, playing games on our phone, and watching movies.

But when the plane arrived at Calgary, it didn't land. Rather, it circled the airport. Then it circled the airport again, and again. Just as we became concerned that we might miss our connecting flight, the pilot announced that he was unable to land due to a violent storm on the ground. He asked for our patience and reassured us that he would land the aircraft once it was safe to do so, and only when it was safe to do so.

We were grateful that someone at the helm knew what was best and had our best interests at heart. We could do nothing about it except sit and wait.

The Waiting Room

When the plane eventually landed and we disembarked, we were shocked at what we saw. The devastating effects of the storm could be seen throughout the airport. Planes had been severely damaged by hail, windows were broken, and thousands of people were milling around because their planes had been unable to take off.

As expected, our connecting flight to Comox was cancelled and airline personnel were unable to tell us when the next flight would be leaving. We had no choice but to wait for our flight to be rescheduled.

The airport was extremely busy. People lined up outside restaurants in hopes of buying coffees, donuts, and other food. Before long, the food was gone. No promises were made as to when trucks would get through to the airport to deliver more.

In the middle of the chaos, Jake approached an airport "official" to ask where we might stretch out for the night. The gentleman loudly verbalized that he couldn't give us permission to stay at the airport. Then he leaned closer, winked his eye, and whispered, "There are benches on the second floor." We decided to spend the night on the second floor of the airport.

Amazingly, I had a set of sheets in my backpack which had been intended to be inserted in our sleeping bags once we arrived at our campsite. We spread them out across some waiting room benches, used our sweatshirts as pillows, and hunkered down for the night.

Before long, others joined our sleeping area. Some stretched out on benches; others slept on the floor.

Although we were frustrated about this delay, we admitted that waiting was better than landing in a hailstorm.

In the end, it all worked out. Our connecting flight to Comox did leave the following day. Our children and grandchildren met us at the airport, and we drove with them to a beautiful and enchanting park at the bottom of a steep hill. Its dense forest of massive and magnificent fir and red cedar trees stretched their needled branches over the park like a canopy, creating a cool and somewhat damp environment for ferns, wildflowers, and a variety of wild animals, including the black bear.

Waiting had been a good thing.

But we wondered, was it good for us to have to wait for Jake to be healed?

As we considered this question, we realized that the waiting had helped us lean in and trust God, the pilot of our plane. We had to believe that He had Jake's best interests at heart.

We waited while we tried to trust.

We trusted while we waited.

SERVING OTHERS WHILE WAITING

MY MOTHER ALWAYS told me that the best way to a man's heart was through his stomach. That was absolutely true when it came to Jake. He loved to eat. He naturally had his favourite foods, like homemade pasta smothered with onions, bacon and sausage. He even believed that some foods paired best with other foods. For example, brown bread definitely paired with homemade green bean soup with Italian garlic sausage.

Jake also loved to eat in restaurants and often talked about the quality of a French onion soup he enjoyed at an upper-class restaurant in the city.

Several days before our local agricultural fair, Jake anticipated ordering a sausage on a bun with a poutine from one of the food trucks.

"I can't wait!" he said to me.

Days later, the smells of garlic and pepper wafted in the air while he savoured every bite of his meal. I could almost taste it.

Even though Jake lost nearly twenty-five pounds during his battle with prostate cancer, he never lost his appetite.

I sometimes wondered whether it was his own love of food that prompted Jake's passion to feed the hungry. A number of years before his diagnosis, Jake heard about the Southwestern Ontario Gleaners (SOG), a new organization in the town nearest to us.

The Gleaners are a not-for-profit charity whose mandate is to convert unmarketable produce into dehydrated vegetable mix and fruit snacks. The finished product is distributed free of charge to hunger relief agencies locally, nationally, and internationally.

People from several area churches had envisioned the Gleaners and donated tens of thousands of dollars towards its inception. Local farmers have since donated produce every year. The washed onions, carrots, potatoes, and peppers are sorted, diced, and dehydrated for three hours before being packaged in three-pound bags of soup mix. Once rehydrated, each bag can feed approximately one hundred people.

By 2022, the Gleaners had produced 4.2 million meals to be distributed to those in need.[12]

One day, Jake's curiosity prompted him to stop by to inquire whether they needed volunteers.

"We're confident that once we're fully up and running, the volunteers will come," the president of the Gleaners told him during a brief tour of the facility. "But we can't open our doors yet because we're in need of one more thing: a trained forklift driver."

He was certainly caught off-guard when by Jake's excided response. "Well, I have my forklift drivers' certification and am available to help out as much as possible!"

In his role as a farmer, Jake had always loved the privilege he'd been given to feed the hungry, so he saw this as a great opportunity. Jake volunteered at the Gleaners five mornings a week. He was absolutely passionate about the work done there.

Jake was unable to volunteer at the Gleaners while he recuperated from surgery. He missed it. Even when he felt strong enough, he wasn't able to return due to circumstances out of his control.

One day, a man approached me at a book fair and asked whether I was Jake's wife. After I confirmed that I was, he shared that he had volunteered with Jake at the Gleaners.

"We're missing him there!" he said.

He later called Jake and offered to take him to the Gleaners.

God knew. God knew all the details of Jake's life and what he needed.

> You discern my going out and my lying down; you are
> familiar with all my ways. (Psalm 139:3)

Jake returned to the Gleaners the following week. I saw a renewed smile on Jake's face. He felt satisfied by doing his part and fulfilling his passion to feed the hungry. Despite his health concerns, he volunteered two mornings a week.

---

[12] Southwestern Ontario Gleaners, *SWOGleaners.ca*. Date of access: July 2, 2024 (https://swogleaners.ca).

Jake filled his time with this good thing.
While he waited.

> For I was hungry and you gave me something to eat...
> Then the righteous will answer him, "Lord, when did we see you hungry and feed you?"
> ...The King will reply, "Truly I tell you, whatever you did for one of the least of these brothers and sisters of mine, you did for me." (Matthew 25:35, 37, 40)

WAITING FOR GOD

WE HAD REPEATEDLY heard the doctor say: "Watch and wait." We also believed that the Lord answered our prayer for healing by saying "Wait." We were waiting on Him and His intervention.

But we wondered whether God waits—and if so, what or who was He waiting for? Then we discovered this verse:

> Yet the Lord longs to be gracious to you; therefore he will rise up to show you compassion. For the Lord is a God of justice. Blessed are all who wait for him! (Isaiah 30:18)

The New American Standard Bible reads a bit differently: "How blessed are all those who long for Him" (Isaiah 30:18, NASB). It became amazingly clear that He longs to be gracious to us, to have compassion on us. And we are blessed when we long for Him.

When Jake and I were dating, we typically only saw each other on the weekends due to the fact that our homes were an hour apart. During the week, we looked forward to seeing each other. When we did see each other, we didn't want our time together to end. We wanted it to last as long as we could. It was also true that between these times together we longed to see each other again. There was an anticipation and expectancy. Of course, the closer we grew to each other, the greater that anticipation and expectancy became.

God waits for us with this same type of longing. He can't wait to see us again! Of course, God's longing for us is intensified a millionfold. Although that may be my own exaggeration, I say it to make a point: since we can't think like God thinks, we also can't understand the depth of His longing for us.

God waits for us, longing for us with great expectation. Why? So He can be gracious to us, show us His compassion, and have a relationship with us.

We see evidence of this in Peter's first letter:

> ...to those once were disobedient long ago when God waited patiently in the days of Noah while the ark was being built. In it only a few people, eight in all, were saved through the water... (1 Peter 3:20)

God waited and longed for others who might come to their senses and join Noah and his family in the ark. It likely took Noah many decades to build the ark. As such, there was ample time and opportunity for people to enter the ark when it was finished and the rains came.

During that time, God waited. Patiently.

God doesn't want "anyone to perish, but everyone to come to repentance" (2 Peter 3:9).

He waits for us. He longs for us. He lingers with expectation. He waits for us to come to Him. He waits for us to repent, to do the right thing, to run to Him and seek His arms of love.

Jake and I reflected further on Isaiah 30:18: "How blessed are all those who long for Him" (NASB). It made us wonder whether we long to be with Him. When we're in His presence, do we linger there? Is the time we spend with Him so rich that we just don't want it to come to an end?

Yes. God waits. God waits for us.

God longs to be with us. He lingers with expectation.

Do we linger with Him?

For just a little while longer?

> Prayer: Thank You, Lord Jesus, for being a gracious God and for wanting to spend time with us. Remind us to linger in your presence. In Jesus's name, amen.

WAITING TIME IS DOUBLING TIME

> Since ancient times no one has heard, no ear has perceived, no eye has seen any God besides you, who acts on behalf of those who wait for him. (Isaiah 64:4)

WHEN OUR GIRLS were teenagers, they at times sought permission to stay late after school for events, or to go to a friend's house. Occasionally, two girls came together to seek permission to do something, or to talk about something that was on their minds.

When Jake and I were approached by two girls together, we knew they really meant business.

"Oh no," we would declare to each other. "Double trouble!"

At times, however, all three girls came at once. There was nothing worse than getting ganged up on by three teenage girls! Triple trouble!

When Jake was on androgen deprivation therapy, the hormone did its job by lowering his testosterone and thus removing the food the cancer needed to grow.

We both understood the reasons for the doctor's recommendation to temporarily take Jake off the hormone therapy, but we felt angst. Once again, the plan was to watch and wait.

We waited and we watched.

Three months after Jake's last hormone shot, the bloodwork showed no change in Jake's PSA and only a slight increase in Jake's testosterone level.

Six months following his last hormone shot, the bloodwork showed a slight increase again in the testosterone, but the PSA remained low.

Around this point in time, we noticed an increase in Jake's energy level. This was understandable given that testosterone gives a man his energy. He was able to do his chores again and enjoy his day without feeling exhausted.

By the ninth month following his last hormone shot, the bloodwork showed a much larger increase in Jake's testosterone level. At the same time, his PSA was still low.

The doctor was very pleased by this. "The PSA is considered almost undetectable."

We were absolutely thrilled by this news. It felt like Jake had been given extra innings in this game called life.

The doctor continued to place him in a watch and wait pattern: wait three months, do more bloodwork, and watch the results. We knew the pattern. But it often felt like we were doing more waiting and very little watching.

Twelve months following his last hormone injection, there was an increase in Jake's PSA. Dr. King indicated that he was concerned; he saw this as an indication that was cancer beginning to rear its ugly head again.

"Let's wait another three months before reintroducing the androgen deprivation therapy," he said.

He then explained that this would allow a second set of PSA numbers to determine the "doubling time." The doubling time was basically the amount of time it took for the PSA level to double. Should the doubling time be greater than six months, the cancer would be considered to be low risk. Less than six months and the cancer would be deemed more aggressive.

Our understanding was that this would help determine the next form of treatment.

Jake shared that it felt nerve-wracking to wait another three months. It scared him, knowing that cancer was floating around in his body and nothing was being done to extinguish it. He was concerned about giving the cancer more opportunity to wreak havoc.

The doctor reassured us. "Waiting another three months won't put you at risk because the PSA is still relatively low. Rather, it will give me the additional information I need in order to substantiate putting you back on hormones."

We agreed to wait.

Three months can feel like an eternity, especially when an important decision needs to be made about your health.

Approximately six weeks prior to having his blood tested again, Jake told me that it felt like this particular three-month period was taking forever to pass. He was worried.

"I just keep wondering where the cancer is and what the PSA will show next time," he confided in me.

I shared his concern. I had been praying that the bloodwork results would be such that the doctor had no doubt regarding the next stage of treatment.

During the ensuing six weeks, we visited all the waiting rooms we had figuratively created in our minds: the waiting rooms of fear and worry, anxiety and wondering. We also often visited God's waiting rooms of trust, patience, perseverance, and grace.

Fifteen months after his last hormone injection, Jake's PSA had risen again. Dr. King explained that when he looked at all the factors, he felt it would be safe to wait an additional three months before restarting hormone therapy.

But Jake was struggling with anxiety and didn't want to wait yet another three months. "Let's zap it now!"

Jake was given an appointment to return the following week for the first in a second series of hormone injections.

We once again made every effort to believe that God was on Jake's side.

While we waited for Him.

> Prayer: Lord, we're scared and feel like we're in a no-win situation. Our hope is that the hormone therapy will once again help, but we absolutely dread the side effects. We do know, though, as You have already promised us, that you will continue to walk with us every step of the way. We praise You and thank You for Your presence in our lives. In Jesus's name we pray, amen.

HERE WE GO AGAIN!

> And the God of all grace, who called you to his eternal glory in Christ, after you have suffered a little while, will himself restore you and make you strong, firm and steadfast. (1 Peter 5:10)

JAKE HAD BEEN given fifteen months to recover from the side effects of the androgen deprivation therapy. Over that time, we noticed his level of energy improve. He felt less exhausted. The mood swings and intense anger were no longer present. In many ways, it felt like my Jacob had been returned to me.

I knew that without the hormone therapy, though, the cancer would spread and potentially wreak havoc in his bones or lymph nodes.

It had been almost exactly five years to the day since we had first sat in Dr. King's waiting room. At that time, I'd had no intention of attending these appointments in five years. I expected that we would receive good news, not bad news!

Yet there we sat. Five years later.

Waiting.

Waiting for Jake's name to be called. Again.

"Jacob Martens!"

We rose together and followed the voice. As we did, I took a deep breath. Here we go again!

My legs felt heavy. It felt like I was lumbering down the hall towards the exam room.

Discouragement taunted me. "Ha! Back on hormone therapy! You prayed and nothing happened! God hasn't healed Jake!"

Yes, we had prayed for healing, and yes, we were still waiting... still waiting for the Lord to intervene.

But while discouragement tried to do its job and claim victory in my spirit, I felt so aware of God's presence and intervention in our lives. As the Creator, He had given us the gift of life. He had also provided doctors, medicine, and knowledge.

Dr. King encouraged us by reminding us that the first round of hormone therapy had done its job, shutting down the testosterone and removing the fuel that the cancer needed to grow. As a result, it had prolonged Jake's life.

In that moment, awareness suddenly smacked me in the face. I realized that God had intervened in this battle. Jake hadn't been "healed," but the hormones were certainly keeping the cancer from progressing to stage four. God had given Jake five more years! He had given us five more years together.

I agreed that it was a good idea to reintroduce the androgen deprivation therapy. I also agreed that it was necessary to prolong Jake's life. But I was scared. I hadn't forgotten how the first round of hormone treatment had changed Jake. I well recalled how difficult it had been to live with his negative and aggressive behaviour.

I shared my trepidation with Dr. King, who explained that Jake's body had responded well to the hormone therapy treatment. Because of the side effects, though, he would likely have to go off it again in about a year's time.

"At that time, we will most likely again see the cancer resurface," Dr. King said. "Which would necessitate Jake going back onto the hormones. This intermittent androgen deprivation therapy will most likely be the pattern for the rest of Jake's life."

Without thinking, I blurted out, "For how long?"

Dr. King was calm and patient. "I don't know the answer to that. He could step outside and get hit by a bus! We just don't know."

I knew the doctor wasn't God. I knew that. None of us know when a person would die. But deep down, I just wanted this cancer to go away!

After we left the office that day, I considered whether there might be some things Jake and I needed to do differently during this next round of hormone injections.

I knew we would both benefit if we became more patient. In that regard, I was fully aware that I grew impatient when overtired. On the other hand,

Jake became more exhausted and impatient due to the hormone therapy. Not a good combination!

We would both need to be intentional about getting more rest.

We had also been made aware that osteoporosis was a side effect of androgen deprivation therapy. Jake needed to take a daily calcium supplement and go for a short walk every day to maintain bone strength. Daily exercise would also assist with his emotional well-being.

Jake had always been strong-willed, but while on the initial round of hormone therapy this had manifested as stubbornness. As stubbornness partnered with anger and exhaustion, it became very difficult to reason with him.

When his second round of hormone therapy started, I recognized that I needed to find ways to let most things go, unless it was an issue of safety.

One day, I found him carrying a soft cushioned dining room chair into the bathroom. His plan was to stand on the chair to change a lightbulb. I supposed he had forgotten that he had fallen off a chair two years earlier.

When I stopped him, feeling it was unsafe for him to stand on the chair, his anger surfaced.

"Look!" He glared at me. "I can stand on a chair if I want to!"

"Yes," I replied calmly. "You are absolutely right. You can. But should you?"

I reminded him that should he fall, he was more prone to break a bone because of the effects of the hormone therapy. Anger and stubbornness joined forces, causing him to argue his case. He wouldn't fall, he insisted. In fact, he demanded that I move out of his way.

I don't know if stubbornness took over my spirit or if it was sheer determination, but either way I held my ground. I believed that this was an issue of safety.

Our eyes met.

"We have a stepladder for the purpose of reaching things over our heads," I said.

At that, he backed down and I returned the chair to the dining room.

I was also determined that I would dismiss Jake's anger and nasty comments and place the blame for his negative behaviour on the hormones.

Due to the long-term complications of surgery, as well as the side effects of hormone therapy, we needed to ensure that we gave each other some loving human touch every day. A hug.

We waited for the hormones to start working.

Prayer: Lord Jesus, we praise You and thank You for intervening in Jake's battle. We are so grateful that You've given us five more years together! As we enter this second round of hormone therapy, please help us to be more loving, kind, and patient while we maintain self-control over our emotions. In Jesus's name we pray, amen.

REGISTER

JAKE HAD ALWAYS been a morning person and been the first one to rise in our household. I would hear him when he got out of bed and watch him go to his dresser, open, the fourth drawer from the top, and pull out a clean pair of jeans. He'd place his left leg into the jeans, followed by his right leg. Once he had pulled his pants up to his waist, he would fasten the button and pull up the zipper. Then he'd retrieved a T-shirt out of the third drawer. Somehow the T-shirt always went on in one fell swoop; his head and both arms would go through the bottom of the shirt while his hands pulled it down over his body. I always marvelled at how quickly that T-shirt went on! Before closing the drawer, he would grab a pair of socks then head down the hallway.

"Morning!" he would call cheerily, waking the girls as he knocked on their bedroom doors. "Get out of bed! It's 6:30!"

Their disgruntled moans were often followed by protests: "Dad! It's only six o'clock! Leave me alone!"

More than four decades later, Jake continued to be the first to rise in the morning. Little had changed in his routine other than the fact that he now sat on the edge of the bed to put on his jeans.

Without realizing it, I think I've always appreciated his routines. They've brought me a sense of the familiar, and in many ways this helps provide a rhythm to my day.

Having had attended so many medical appointments, after a while Jake and I became familiar with the routines of the medical staff. It didn't seem to matter whether he was seeing a doctor or having a test done; the routines at every appointment were basically the same.

First Jake registered with reception. Doing so ensured that someone knew he was in the waiting room. How frustrating it could have been if we'd waited for hours for him to be called in only to find out that the staff hadn't even know he was there!

The Waiting Room

Once registered, we waited. When it was time for him to be seen, someone called his name.

One day Jake pointed out to me that they always used his formal name, as it appeared on his health card: "Jacob Martens."

Once called, we rose and followed the voice to an exam room where the doctor met with us.

These standard practices produced familiarity.

During a period of quiet reflection one morning, it occurred to me that in life we follow similar patterns. We are registered when we're born. We wait in this waiting room called life. Then one day, we hear the Lord call our name, at which time we rise and follow His voice.

When a baby is born in Canada, the parents are required to complete and submit a statement of live birth with the government. In addition, medical staff are required to complete and submit a notice of live birth. Once the government has received both documents, a birth certificate is issued.

When a child is adopted in Canada, a second statement of live birth form is completed showing the names of the adoptive parents. That form is registered on top of the original statement of live birth, as though the adoptive parents were the birth parents.

Canadian citizens are allowed to travel freely in Canada. However, a passport is required to enter another country or gain entrance back into Canada. Based on that birth registration, Canadian citizens can apply for a passport which proves a person's citizenship to the officials of other countries.

When I was preparing to leave on a mission trip, I checked my passport to make certain it had not expired. This prompted Jake to check the expiry date on his passport. In doing so, he discovered that he needed to renew his passport. As a result, he obtained the appropriate passport application and made arrangements to have new passport photos taken.

"What do you think?" he later asked while completing the form. "Should I renew my passport for an additional five years, or ten?"

His question tugged at my heartstrings. Our eyes met. We both knew the deeper meaning behind this question. In that split second, we knew that Jake was facing his own mortality.

Without hesitating, and with as much hope as I could muster, I replied, "Ten years! Of course!"

None of us know when we will die, or when we'll no longer be able to travel. But because ten years was the maximum allowable time for that passport renewal, that's what he chose.

As we reflected on these worldly processes, we remembered that we also had experienced a spiritual registration.

Jake looked back on the faith commitment he had made when he was a teen. He had been raised in a warm and loving Christian home where God and the church had been his family's main focal points. He treasured the vivid memories of his mother kneeling beside her bed, praying. These things spoke to him of the importance of putting his faith in a loving and saving God.

In his later teens, he had recognized that he needed to claim Christianity as his own. So he'd made a personal and individual commitment to the Lord Jesus as his Saviour. He was later baptized upon confession of his faith in Jesus.

Then, in the summer of 1994, during a Sunday morning worship service when the congregation was singing, Jake had experienced a strong encounter with the Holy Spirit. This experience was so powerful that it had caused Jake to break down in tears of joy at the same time that his heart was inundated with gratitude for the awesome power of the Spirit. He had been showered with the gift of faith, which reaffirmed in him that the walk in life he had chosen, the Christian walk, was the right one.

Jake told me that he firmly believed the words Jesus spoke to Nicodemus: "You must be born again... For God so loved the world that he gave his one and only Son, that whoever believes in him shall not perish but have eternal life" (John 3:7, 16).

Jesus loved us so much that He took the penalty for our sins when He died on the cross. When Jake asked Jesus to be his Saviour, he was promised eternal life with Him after death. From that very moment, Jake knew he had become one of God's children.

> Yet to all who did receive him, to those who believed in his name, he gave the right to become children of God—children born not of natural descent, nor of human decision or a husband's will, but born of God. (John 1:12–13)

When Jake asked Jesus to be his Saviour, his spiritual registration as God's child covered over the original birth certificate showing his mother and father as his parents. God adopted Jake as His own child, becoming his Father!

> ...he predestined us for adoption to sonship through Jesus Christ, in accordance with his pleasure and will... (Ephesians 1:5)

Furthermore, Paul tells us:

> But our citizenship is in heaven. And we eagerly await a Savior from there, the Lord Jesus Christ, who, by the power that enables him to bring everything under his control, will transform our lowly bodies so that they will be like his glorious body. (Philippians 3:20–21)

Jake received his passport to heaven and his name has been written there in the book of life. Jake has been adopted as God's child and his citizenship is in heaven.

> ...rejoice that your names are written in heaven. (Luke 10:20)

Prayer: Lord Jesus, we are humbled that You were willing to die for us and that You have written our names in the book of life. Thank you for adopting us as Your children. In Jesus's name we pray, amen.

WAIT

REGISTER.

Wait.

Since Jake's battle with prostate cancer began, we waited in so many waiting rooms. From the moment he registered for the first time, we waited.

As we waited, we occupied ourselves. We replied to emails, read the news, and played games on our phones. Sometimes we tried to relax, and other times we took the time to pray. Still other times, we observed others and listened to their conversations. These distractions filled the waiting time.

Between appointments, we visited our figurative waiting rooms where we vacillated between faith and fear. We knew that God sat with us in those waiting rooms. We also knew that we could go to Him at any time and He would listen and comfort us. In addition, we also sat in God's waiting room, where He asked us to wait for His intervention; there, we waited for Him and with Him.

We recognized that those figurative waiting rooms and God's waiting room collectively belong to a much larger waiting room: the waiting room called life—the span of time between when we're born and when we die. When strung together, these moments turn into hours, then days, then months, then years, and then a lifetime. And while we live life, we collected these moments, emotions, and experiences.

Everyone has been given a different span of time. For some, it's just a breath. For others, it lasts a century or more. For Jake, it had already been seventy-four years. We hoped for many more years to come.

In the four-step process of register, wait, hear your name, and follow the voice, the longest has definitely been wait. We ask ourselves, what is life? What do we do? What have we done while in that waiting room called life?

Certainly, Solomon, the author of Ecclesiastes, had his own slant on life. He wrote, "Utterly meaningless! Everything is meaningless" (Ecclesiastes 1:2).

The first time Jake read through Ecclesiastes, he was taken aback by Solomon's idea of life and its futility. For Solomon, everything seemed meaningless, including work and pleasures. By the end of the book, he summarized life this way:

> Now all has been heard; here is the conclusion of the matter: fear God and keep his commandments, for this is the duty of all mankind. (Ecclesiastes 12:13)

King David seemed to highlight the same sentiment:

> Show me, Lord, my life's end and the number of my days; let me know how fleeting my life is. You have made my days a mere handbreadth; the span of my years is as nothing before you. Everyone is but a breath, even those who seem secure (Psalm 39:4–5).

When Jake reflected on this so-called meaninglessness of life in Ecclesiastes, and how fleeting life is in the Psalms, he felt sad for the authors. He saw life as a gift, an opportunity to have a relationship with Jesus.

When God created Adam and Eve, He wanted a relationship with mankind. When they disobeyed Him and ate from the fruit of the tree (Genesis 3:6), they heard God walking in the garden. They hid.

> But the Lord God called to the man, "Where are you?"
> (Genesis 3:9)

God knew they had disobeyed Him and their punishment was separation from Him. But as a God of compassion, He sent His son Jesus to bridge the chasm over mankind's sin in order to restore the relationship between man and God.

In the midst of life's struggles, and in particular in the middle of this battle with cancer, Jake continued to hope in the One who gave him life.

"Can you imagine how difficult this waiting room called life would be if I didn't know the Lord or have a relationship with Jesus?" Jake calmly said to me one day. "Without that, life would have been much more difficult, and certainly meaningless!"

As much as Jake believed that, he had to work at not falling into the traps of futility and meaninglessness. It became necessary for him to spend time in the positive waiting rooms of prayer and praise.

However, staying in those positive waiting rooms wasn't easy. It wasn't easy because life wasn't easy. But we knew that God had promised us, despite all of the struggles in life, that He would give us a garment of praise (Isaiah 61:3).

In the meantime, we rest in this waiting room called life. But it's not a rest as in doing nothing. Rather it's a restful peace knowing that one day He will call us home. In fact, while in this waiting room we have worked, loved, and served others. And we served Him while we expectantly waited.

As had been our experience thirty years prior to cancer, and six weeks before Jake's prostatectomy, we waited in line at Disney World for up to two hours to get on a ride. But nobody seemed to mind because there was a quiet understanding that Disney World didn't have any bad rides. Knowing that made the wait tolerable.

Likewise, while we waited in this waiting room called life, including its joys, sorrows, and suffering, we waited eagerly for God to call us home to heaven. We waited expectantly with a longing to be reunited with our Saviour. We waited while knowing that, in the end, it will be worth the wait.

We continue to wait.

WHAT ARE WE WAITING FOR?

DR. KING REPEATEDLY referred to a wait-and-watch pattern.

While in this waiting room called life, we realized that we were also in a wait-and-watch pattern. We asked ourselves, what were we watching for? What were we waiting for?

Jesus told some of His disciples that one day He would return:

> But about that day or hour no one knows, not even the angels in heaven, nor the Son, but only the Father. Be on guard! Be alert! You do not know when that time will come. It's like a man going away: He leaves his house and puts his servants in charge, each with their assigned task, and tells the one at the door to keep watch.
>
> Therefore keep watch because you do not know when the owner of the house will come back—whether in the evening, or at midnight, or when the rooster crows, or at dawn. If he comes suddenly, do not let him find you sleeping. What I say to you, I say to everyone: "Watch!" (Mark 13:32–37)

In the Scriptures, James also encourages us to watch for the Lord's return.

> Be patient, then, brothers and sisters, until the Lord's coming. See how the farmer waits for the land to yield its valuable crop, patiently waiting for the autumn and spring rains. You too, be patient and stand firm, because the Lord's coming is near. (James 5:7–8)

The Waiting Room

We had to admit that we weren't waiting to die. Rather, we were watching while we lived. We were watching for the Lord to return, watching for Him to gather His children, to meet Him, to be with Him forever.

> After that, we who are still alive and are left will be caught up together with them in the clouds to meet the Lord in the air. And so we will be with the Lord forever. (1 Thessalonians 4:17)

Then, when we arrive in heaven to be with Jesus forever, we will sing praises to the Lord for all He has done:

> "Holy, holy, holy is the Lord God Almighty," who was, and is, and is to come. (Revelation 4:8)

Ultimately, we watch and wait for Him to return.
We watch for Him.
We watch while we wait.

HEAR YOUR NAME

> But now, this is what the Lord says—he who created you, Jacob, he who formed you, Israel: "Do not fear, for I have redeemed you; I have summoned you by name; you are mine. When you pass through the waters, I will be with you; and when you pass through the rivers, they will not sweep over you. When you walk through the fire, you will not be burned; the flames will not set you ablaze. For I am the Lord your God, the Holy One of Israel, your Savior...
> (Isaiah 43:1–3)

WE WAIT FOR Him to call our name. This will happen at our appointed time, or when we meet Him in the air to live with Him for all eternity.

Not long after Jake's diagnosis, I had a quiet time with the Lord. Even though we didn't yet have a prognosis, I still wept. I shared with the Lord that I wasn't ready for Him to call Jake home. That's when I heard the Lord tell me He would call Jake's name one day.

Even before Jake was born, God knew all about him because He created him, and He knew exactly how many days had been established for the length of Jake's life.

> My frame was not hidden from you when I was made in the secret place, when I was woven together in the depths of the earth. Your eyes saw my unformed body; all the days ordained for me were written in your book before one of them came to be. (Psalm 139:15–16)

At the moment Jake asked Jesus to be his Saviour, his name was registered in the book of life.

Now he waits. In hopeful waiting, he tarries and longs for the Father who has adopted him as His own, to redeem his body.

> Not only so, but we ourselves, who have the firstfruits of the Spirit, groan inwardly as we wait eagerly for our adoption to sonship, the redemption of our bodies. For in this hope we were saved. But hope that is seen is no hope at all. Who hopes for what they already have? But if we hope for what we do not yet have, we wait for it patiently. (Romans 8:23–25)

One day God will call Jake's name. At the appointed time He has already established, He will call Jake's name. I've heard Jake's name called many times by nurses, technicians, or clerks. I can still hear their voices in my memory. But when God calls Jake's name, he will meet up with his Saviour in heaven.

I don't know what the Lord's actual voice sounds like. But I can imagine Him calling "Jacob Martens!" I can't bear the thought of it, the thought of being separated from him. My spirit breaks when I even consider that the Lord will one day call Jake's name. But in the middle of that pain, I am comforted in knowing that Jake will go to be with Jesus. Once with Jesus, he won't have any more worry or sorrow, no fear for tomorrow, because he will be with Jesus.

Of course, we have no idea which one of us will be called home first. But we do know that when He calls our names, either separately or together, we will be united with our Saviour in heaven. When we arrive there, it will be glorious!

> "He will wipe every tear from their eyes. There will be no more death" or mourning or crying or pain, for the old order of things has passed away. (Revelation 21:4)

We held onto that hope.

"I believe God's got it!" Jake told me one day. "Should I be healed and live a longer life yet, then God's got that. He's in control. But should I die from cancer, whenever that might be, then God's got that, too. Either way, I am healed!"

God's got it!

FOLLOW MY VOICE

REGISTER.
> Wait.
> Hear your name.
> Follow the voice.
> "Jacob Martens."

Jake's name had been called many times. Each and every time he heard his name called, he stood and followed the voice.

When the Lord Jesus eventually calls Jake's name, he won't follow the voice across the hall, down a hallway, and into an exam room. Rather, he will follow the voice of his Saviour. Why? Because Jake knows the sound of His Saviour's voice.

In his gospel, John gave us a beautiful picture of Jesus as the good Shepherd. His sheep are described as those who believe in Him, those He calls His children. The Shepherd leads the sheep and protects them from predatory animals. The sheep know that the Shepherd loves them, cares for them, and wants the best for them. So when they hear His voice, they follow Him.

> The gatekeeper opens the gate for him, and the sheep listen to his voice. He calls his own sheep by name and leads them out. When he has brought out all his own, he goes on ahead of them, and his sheep follow him because they know his voice. (John 10:3–4)

> Therefore Jesus said again, "Very truly I tell you, I am the gate for the sheep. All who have come before me are thieves and robbers, but the sheep have not listened to them. I am the gate; whoever enters through me will be saved." (John 10:7–90)

The Waiting Room

> That good Shepherd, Jesus, gave His life for His sheep.

> My sheep listen to my voice; I know them, and they follow me. I give them eternal life, and they shall never perish; no one will snatch them out of my hand. (John 10:27–28)

My brother, David, died in 2014. Prior to his death, when his wife and son were helping him readjust himself in bed one day, David appeared startled and pointed to the ceiling.

"The light," he said, taking a deep breath. "The light is so beautiful!"

He started to shake. With tears rolling down his cheeks, he lowered his head and became quiet, totally in awe of what he had experienced.

The Lord continued to open heaven up to David.

I was present when my mother died in 1981. While in a coma, my siblings and I watched and waited as Jesus Christ opened up heaven to her. She expressed amazement at what she saw.

"Wow! Awe! It's so beautiful!"

Several hours later, she again expressed wonder and amazement over the beautiful things she'd seen and heard. A sense of peace filled the room. Serenity enshrouded her face.

Two days later, my mother took her last breath.

In Acts, we read that the Sanhedrin was furious with Stephen for challenging them about being so stiff-necked.

> But Stephen, full of the Holy Spirit, looked up to heaven and saw the glory of God, and Jesus standing at the right hand of God. "Look," he said, "I see heaven open and the Son of Man standing at the right hand of God." (Acts 7:55–56)

Heaven was opened up to Stephen: "While they were stoning him, Stephen prayed, 'Lord Jesus, receive my spirit'" (Acts 7:59).

From these experiences and from the Scripture, I was comforted in knowing that Jake would one day hear Christ call his name and that he would rise and follow the voice of his Shepherd.

I have imagined the Lord calling Jake's name. I have imagined Jake hearing His voice. I have wept at the thought of him leaving me. But I know that he will be with the Saviour.

> I know that my redeemer lives, and that in the end he will stand on the earth. And after my skin has been destroyed, yet in my flesh I will see God; I myself will see him with my own eyes—I, and not another. How my heart yearns within me! (Job 19:25–27)

This is when all of Jake's faith will fall into place. His relationship with Jesus, love for his Saviour, trust in Him no matter what, and belief that God's got it will come together at the finish line he's been running towards. Because at the end of the race, at the end of the waiting, at the end of waiting in this place called life, God will call Jake home to be with Him in heaven.

Forever.

> I press on toward the goal to win the prize for which God has called me heavenward in Christ Jesus. (Philippians 3:14)

I imagine that glorious day when Jake is called and follows the voice of Jesus. I imagine him joining Jesus in heaven. I imagine when he arrives at the gates of heaven! I imagine Jake falling at the Lord's feet and hearing His voice as the Lord speaks to him.

> When I saw him, I fell at his feet as though dead. Then he placed his right hand on me and said: "Do not be afraid. I am the First and the Last. I am the Living One; I was dead, and now look, I am alive for ever and ever!" (Revelation 1:17–18)

Can you imagine this for yourself? Just imagine following the voice of Jesus here on earth, as your good Shepherd. Then, because you know that

The Waiting Room

voice so well, when He calls your name, you follow Him! Imagine falling at His feet and hearing His loving voice as He speaks to you.

Just imagine!

STILL WAITING

EARLY ONE MORNING, Jake woke me and said, "I think you should end the book now, while we're still in the waiting."

At first it seemed unfair to the reader not to tell the rest of Jake's story. But when I reflected on his suggestion, it occurred to me that Jake's story will go one of two ways.

Jake will either die of prostate cancer or from some other cause. In either case, the Lord will call his name and Jake will follow Him home.

Or the Lord will return in the twinkling of an eye, just as He has promised, and Jake will meet Jesus in the air and be taken home to heaven.

> Listen, I tell you a mystery: We will not all sleep, but we will all be changed—in a flash, in the twinkling of an eye, at the last trumpet. (1 Corinthians 15:51–52)

Either way, Jake will be healed.

Meanwhile, we wait.

We wait in God's waiting room where He is present with us every step of the way.

We wait in the waiting room called life.

We wait for Him to call our name.

We wait with great expectation.

> I wait for the Lord, my whole being waits, and in his word I put my hope. (Psalm 130:5)

POSTSCRIPT

"PROSTATE CANCER CHANGED my life," Jake said to me one day. "Even though for the most part we live in the unknown, there are times when we can change things, or make things right, or do something about the situation we're in. But cancer! Cancer had the ability to put me in that place of the unknown where I couldn't do anything about it, and I certainly couldn't change it."

Jake's once active and strong body became weaker as he battled this disease. He needed more sleep. He struggled with the long-term complications from surgery and radiation, and the androgen deprivation therapy took a toll on his body and emotions.

But as his body became weaker, Jake's faith in Jesus remained strong.

"It feels like we live our lives three months at a time," he remarked. "It often feels like forever. Always wondering, sometimes worrying, always waiting, trying to trust. I have to believe that whatever plan the Lord has for me, it's something I will trust Him for. God didn't create robots, He created us with minds of our own. There's nothing I can do about having cancer, but I can trust Him while I'm in the struggle and know, truly know, that the Lord still has a plan for me."

He then quoted his favourite Bible verse: "'For I know the plans I have for you,' declares the Lord, 'plans to prosper you and not to harm you, plans to give you hope and a future'" (Jeremiah 29:11).

When he finished, he admitted that his feelings were conflicted.

"If God really has plans to not harm me, then why do I have to go through all of this?" Almost immediately he resolved that question with the promise that God had given him a hope and a future. "It may not be here on earth, but it will be a glorious hope and future."

Even though our family had lost several members to cancer, we hadn't been prepared to deal with this disease. We had prepared for many other

The Waiting Room

things in our lives, including our children, budgets, the farm equipment we needed, and saving for vacations, retirement, and even illness, to name just a few. But we hadn't prepared for hearing a diagnosis of cancer, or how to share the news with others, and thankfully so.

Since Jake's battle with prostate cancer began, we have vacillated between trusting God and doubting Him. Many times we felt lost and overwhelmed. Our deepest desire was for cancer to go away and for Jake to be totally well again. I longed for him to have restored energy. I longed for him to not be reliant upon the hormone therapy as a means of survival. I longed for him to be healed.

It goes without saying that Jake had many medical appointments, and as such we sat in many waiting rooms. Between those appointments, we waited for the next appointment, or the next test, or the next form of treatment. Oftentimes the wait was frustrating and painful.

As a result, we created waiting rooms in our own minds where we buckled under the weight of discouragement and faced the reality of this disease.

But whenever we found ourselves in those difficult waiting rooms, the Lord Jesus repeatedly turned our faces to look to Him as He ministered to us through His written Word and invited us to join Him in the waiting rooms called hope, prayer, trust, perseverance, praise, and grace.

Throughout his battle, we recalled the many positive experiences we had in life when the Lord was faithful to us. This regularly helped us refocus our attention to our God, who is faithful, trustworthy, forgiving, gracious, and the embodiment of love and hope.

We learned that it was okay to cry and mourn our losses. It was all right to ask the doctors questions. Lots of them. It was okay to ask others to pray for Jake. We learned anew how much we valued those prayers.

We learned that our happiness wasn't based on those things that happening around us, for we could find joy even in the middle of our difficulties.

We learned that it was okay to tell God exactly what we felt, because we were certain He had broad shoulders and could handle it.

We also learned new things about God. We learned that He keeps His promises. He told me that He would walk with me every step of the way, and He did. He never left us alone.

Postscript

"I learned that I couldn't tell God what to do," Jake said to me one day. "I've learned that I had to trust Him while I believed He had my back, that He's in control and has our best interests in mind—all the time!"

As long and hard as the battle has already been, Jake has persevered. We have persevered together, never stopped praying, and kept fighting while we hoped.

We have experienced this waiting room called life. When the waiting is over, we will finally be reunited with Jesus and be able to say that the wait was worth it.

Writing this book has given me the opportunity to consider this man I have been married to for forty-six years. In those reflections, I fully recognized and understood how important his relationship with the Lord Jesus is to him. As I prayed for Jake, cared for him, and continued to care about him, I felt a closer emotional intimacy with him that I ever felt before.

I cannot even begin to empathize with those who have already lost a spouse. In that regard, should the Lord decide to call Jake home before me, I have no idea of the pain I will face as I enter the darkness of grief.

But I do know this: I have hope. Just as Jesus walked with me every step of the way through Jake's struggle with prostate cancer, I have hope that He will also walk with me through that grief. At that time, He will hold me, hug me, and minister to me through His love and through the love of others.

One day I told our youngest daughter that I had deeply struggled with cancer being referred to as a "journey."

She responded with words of encouragement: "It's not about the journey, Mom. It's about the destination."

Ultimately, a person's life as a whole is a journey. As Jesus-followers, the end destination will take us to heaven where we will be reunited with Jesus, and with one another.

Hopefully we will meet you there, too.

Until then, we wait.

The Waiting Room

> I will extol the Lord at all times;
> his praise will always be on my lips.
> I will glory in the Lord;
> let the afflicted hear and rejoice.
> Glorify the Lord with me;
> let us exalt his name together.
> (Psalm 34:1–3)

ABOUT THE AUTHOR

DARLENE MARTENS AND her husband Jake have been married for more than forty-six years and continue to live in southwestern Ontario. She is a graduate from the University of Windsor with a Master of Social Work. In addition, she holds a Bachelor of Social Work from the University of Manitoba and a Bachelor of Arts in Social Development Studies from the University of Waterloo. She is registered with the Ontario College of Social Workers and Social Service Workers (OCSWSSW) and with the Ontario Association of Social Workers (OASW). She currently works as a social worker/therapist.

Darlene is an international speaker and has spoken at several women's conferences. She has also served in a variety of roles in the church, including teaching Sunday school and serving as a deacon. Her passion is to see others put their faith in Jesus Christ as their Saviour and to seek Him for healing.

You can contact Darlene by emailing her at martensddd@gmail.com or by visiting www.darlenemartensauthor.com.

Amazing Grace, Abounding Love
978-1-4866-1703-6

FEELING ALONE AND afraid, six-year-old Darlene hides under the porch, crying. When her sister finds her, Darlene is unable to explain the fear she faces at nighttime.

Later, as a wife and a mother, she processes the impact of the sexual abuse while struggling with depression. Through this deep emotional pain, she recognizes that Christ has already won the victory over Satan. But can she forgive her father? And can she find peace as she sets out to learn the truth about her biological mother?